DISCARD

Teen Pregnancy

JENNIFER A. HURLEY

Greenhaven Press, Inc., San Diego, California

Library of Congress Cataloging-in-Publication Data

Hurley, Jennifer A., 1973–
    Teen pregnancy/Jennifer A. Hurley
        p.   cm. — (Opposing viewpoints digests)
    Includes bibliographical references and index.
    Summary: Examines the differing viewpoints on issues related to teen pregnancy, including factors that contribute to this problem, its effects on teenagers' lives, and possible ways to prevent teen pregnancy.
    ISBN 0-7377-0365-2 (pbk. : alk. paper)—ISBN 0-7377-366-0 (lib. bdg. : alk. paper)
    1. Teenage pregnancy—United States—Juvenile literature. [1. Pregnancy.] I. Title. II. Series.
HQ759.4 .H87 2000
306.874'3—dc21   00-037135

Cover Photo: © Uniphoto Picture Agency
Digital Stock, Children & Teens, 24
© Caroline Penn/Corbis, 28
PhotoDisc, Vol. 46, Beauty and Health, 48
PhotoDisc, Vol. 24, Education, 40
Martha Schierholz, 19
© Jennie Woodcock; Reflections Photolibrary/Corbis, 33

© 2000 by Greenhaven Press, Inc.
PO Box 289009, San Diego, CA 92198-9009

Printed in the U.S.A.

CONTENTS

FOREWORD

The only way in which a human being can make some approach to knowing the whole of a subject is by hearing what can be said about it by persons of every variety of opinion and studying all modes in which it can be looked at by every character of mind. No wise man ever acquired his wisdom in any mode but this.

—John Stuart Mill

Today, young adults are inundated with a wide variety of points of view on an equally wide spectrum of subjects. Often overshadowing traditional books and newspapers as forums for these views are a host of broadcast, print, and electronic media, including television news and entertainment programs, talk shows, and commercials; radio talk shows and call-in lines; movies, home videos, and compact discs; magazines and supermarket tabloids; and the increasingly popular and influential Internet.

For teenagers, this multiplicity of sources, ideas, and opinions can be both positive and negative. On the one hand, a wealth of useful, interesting, and enlightening information is readily available virtually at their fingertips, underscoring the need for teens to recognize and consider a wide range of views besides their own. As Mark Twain put it, "It were not best that we should all think alike; it is difference of opinion that makes horse races." On the other hand, the range of opinions on a given subject is often too wide to absorb and analyze easily. Trying to keep up with, sort out, and form personal opinions from such a barrage can be daunting for anyone, let alone young people who have not yet acquired effective critical judgment skills.

Moreover, to the task of evaluating this assortment of impersonal information, many teenagers bring firsthand experience of serious and emotionally charged social and health problems, including divorce, family violence, alcoholism and drug abuse, rape, unwanted pregnancy, the spread of AIDS, and eating disorders. Teens are often forced to deal with these problems before they are capable of objective opinion based on reason and judgment. All too often, teens' response to these deep personal issues is impulsive rather than carefully considered.

Greenhaven Press's Opposing Viewpoints Digests are designed to aid in examining important current issues in a way that develops critical thinking and evaluating skills. Each book presents thought-provoking argument and stimulating debate on a single issue. By examining an issue from many different points of view, readers come to realize its complexity and acknowledge the validity of opposing opinions. This insight is especially helpful in writing reports, research papers, and persuasive essays, when students must competently address common objections and controversies related to their topic. In addition, examination of the diverse mix of opinions in each volume challenges readers to question their own strongly held opinions and assumptions. While the point of such examination is not to change readers' minds, examining views that oppose their own will certainly deepen their own knowledge of the issue and help them realize exactly why they hold the opinion they do.

The Opposing Viewpoints Digests offer a number of unique features that sharpen young readers' critical thinking and reading skills. To assure an appropriate and consistent reading level for young adults, all essays in each volume are written by a single author. Each essay heavily quotes readable primary sources that are fully cited to allow for further research and documentation. Thus, primary sources are introduced in a context to enhance comprehension.

In addition, each volume includes extensive research tools. A section containing relevant source material includes interviews, excerpts from original research, and the opinions of prominent spokespersons. A "facts about" section allows students to peruse relevant facts and statistics; these statistics are also fully cited, allowing students to question and analyze the credibility of the source. Two bibliographies, one for young adults and one listing the author's sources, are also included; both are annotated to guide student research. Finally, a comprehensive index allows students to scan and locate content efficiently.

Greenhaven's Opposing Viewpoints Digests, like Greenhaven's higher level and critically acclaimed Opposing Viewpoints Series, have been developed around the concept that an awareness and appreciation for the complexity of seemingly simple issues is particularly important in a democratic society. In a democracy, the common good is often, and very appropriately, decided by open debate of widely varying views. As one of our democracy's greatest advocates, Thomas Jefferson, observed, "Difference of opinion leads to inquiry, and inquiry to truth." It is to this principle that Opposing Viewpoints Digests are dedicated.

Teen Pregnancy and Society's Changing Values About Sex

According to the Alan Guttmacher Institute, 97 of every 1,000 girls aged 15 to 19 become pregnant each year in the United States. Although this rate is approximately 12 percent lower than the 1990 rate, it is still more than twice that of any other industrialized nation in the world. In the Netherlands, for example, the percentage of teens who become pregnant is just 7 of every 1,000 girls.

However, it is not the actual number of pregnant teens that inspires such concern over the problem of teen pregnancy. Compared to the 1960s, in fact, a smaller percentage of teens are becoming pregnant. What worries contemporary social critics is that the vast majority of teen pregnancies—71 percent as of 1996—are to *unmarried* teenagers.

In some ways, the rise in unwed pregnancy among teens is only a mirror of similar changes in adult behavior. Douglas Kirby, author of *No Easy Answers: Research Findings on Programs to Reduce Teen Pregnancy* maintains that "trends among adolescents have paralleled similar trends among older adults. Over time, older adults have also engaged in a greater amount of sex outside of marriage and their out-of-wedlock birth rate has risen. When the birth rate for adults . . . rises or falls, the birth rate for adolescents typically does the same."[1]

Changing Values About Sex

Teens, like adults, are more likely now than in the past to have premarital sex and, as a result, to bear children out of wedlock. By the time teenagers reach the age of sixteen, 39 percent of females and 45 percent of males are sexually active; by the age of nineteen, the percentages are as high as 77 for females and 85 for males.

In general, such shifts in sexual behavior reflect widespread changes in societal values about sexuality. The sexual revolution of the 1960s, a movement initiated by some of the same activists working to uphold racial equality and women's rights, challenged the idea that sex was only appropriate within the sphere of marriage. For the first time in history, Americans began to question the traditional moral codes that considered all forms of premarital sex to be wrong.

Thus, over time, a significant number of Americans have come to adopt the view that premarital sex between two committed partners is morally acceptable. As David Whitman, Paul Glastris, and Brendan I. Koener contend,

> Americans, at least tacitly, have all but given up on the notion that the appropriate premarital state is one of chastity. . . . For most . . . , adult premarital sex has become "sin" they not only wink at but quietly endorse. On television, adult virgins are as rare as caribou in Manhattan. . . . A *U.S. News* poll shows that . . . more than half [of Americans] believe it is not at all wrong, or wrong only sometimes, for adults to have premarital sex.[2]

Views About Teen Sex

Yet despite the fact that many adults in American society implicitly condone premarital sex between other adults, they are deeply ambivalent about whether it is acceptable for teenagers to have sex. Kristin Luker, author of *Dubious Conceptions: The Politics of Teen Pregnancy*, explains why so many Americans are uncomfortable with teens having sex:

> Many Americans object to the idea of "casual" sex, meaning sex that is not closely linked to the process by which people form couples and settle down. Yet teenagers, especially young teenagers, are almost universally regarded as too young to "get serious" and contemplate marriage. The kinds of sex that are appropriate for them (short-term relationships for the purpose of pleasure, not procreation) run counter to the basic values espoused by many adults. This double bind, according to which serious commitments are premature but casual sex is immoral, makes sexual activity [among teens] inherently troubling for many adults.[3]

Adults of all political persuasions tend to agree that it is preferable for teenagers to delay sex until adulthood, because the risks of premarital sex—especially with the advent of AIDS—are so high. Beyond this basic level of agreement, however, controversy abounds. Most religious leaders, for example, argue that it is always inappropriate for teens to have sex because premarital sex is inherently unethical. The National Campaign to Prevent Teen Pregnancy (NCPTP) summarizes the view taken by faith traditions: "The sexual act is properly directed toward [the] purpose [of reproduction], which in turn provides the true moral criterion for human sexuality. The good of the child and the law of God both require marriage for the sexual act to be [moral]."[4]

On the other side are those who argue that teen sex, while not necessarily a good thing, is not always problematic. They contend that teenagers, especially older teens, can act with maturity about issues of sex. Columnist Richard Cohen writes that even among teenagers, "There's nothing wrong with responsible sex."[5]

Preventing Teenage Pregnancy

These contrasting ideologies play an important role in the debate about how to prevent teenage pregnancy. Those who believe teenage sex is wrong support programs that advise teens to say no to sex. This is known as abstinence-only sex education. Others advocate comprehensive sex education, which attempts to mitigate the harm teens face if they do engage in sexual activity. These programs teach teens to protect themselves against pregnancy and sexually transmitted diseases by using condoms or other forms of contraception.

The fundamental incompatibility between these two approaches, however, makes it difficult for society to adopt a unified stance on teen pregnancy prevention. As the NCPTP's Task Force on Religion and Public Values asserts, "[Americans] find it easy . . . to compromise when the issue is how a pot of material resources is to be divided. . . . It is much harder to split the

Teenage Pregnancy

▶ The pregnancy rate among sexually experienced teenagers dropped from 254 to 207 per 1,000 (19%) in the last two decades.

▶ 85% of teenage pregnancies are unplanned, accounting for about one-fourth of all accidental pregnancies each year.

▶ Six in ten teenage pregnancies occur among 18- to 19-year-olds.

▶ Among sexually experienced teenagers, about 9% of 14-year-olds, 18% of 15- to 17-year-olds, and 22% of 18- to 19-year-olds become pregnant each year.

▶ Only 26% of the men involved in the pregnancies among women under age 18 are estimated to have been that young.

▶ Teenage pregnancy rates in the United States are twice as high as in England and Wales, France, and Canada; and 9 times as high as in the Netherlands and Japan.

Source: The Alan Guttmacher Institute, 1994.

difference . . . when our basic sense of right and wrong—of what gives meaning and worth to human existence—is at stake."[6]

However, the experience of other industrialized countries, where teen pregnancy is relatively low, suggests that solidarity might be what is needed in order to curb the problem of teenage pregnancy. In Japan, for example, teenagers commonly abstain from sex because it is frowned upon by society. In contrast, Western European countries such as the Netherlands expect that teens will have sex and counsel them openly on matters of birth control. The United States, a society that simultaneously takes both approaches, has met the problem of teen pregnancy with little success. *Teen Pregnancy: Opposing Viewpoints Digests* provides a variety of perspectives on why so many American teenagers become pregnant and what society can do to remedy this troubling problem.

1. Douglas Kirby, *No Easy Answers: Research Findings on Programs to Reduce Teen Pregnancy.* Washington, DC: National Campaign to Prevent Teen Pregnancy, 1997, p. 3.

2. David Whitman, Paul Glastris, and Brendan I. Koener, "Was It Good for Us?" *U.S. News & World Report*, May 19, 1997, pp. 1–2.

3. Kristin Luker, *Dubious Conceptions: The Politics of Teen Pregnancy.* Cambridge, MA: Harvard University Press, 1996, p. 91.

4. National Campaign to Prevent Teen Pregnancy, *While the Adults Are Arguing, the Teens Are Getting Pregnant: Overcoming Conflict in Teen Pregnancy Prevention.* Washington, DC, 1998, p. 4.

5. Richard Cohen, "Sex-Is-Shameful Attitude," *Liberal Opinion Week*, July 5, 1997, p. 15.

6. National Campaign to Prevent Teen Pregnancy, *While the Adults Are Arguing, the Teens Are Getting Pregnant*, p. 4.

CHAPTER 1

How Critical Is the Problem of Teen Pregnancy?

"The rate of pregnancy among unmarried teens skyrocketed during the last half of the twentieth century—and continues to rise."

Teen Pregnancy Causes Serious Harm to Society

Each year, 1 million American teenagers—10 percent of all girls aged fifteen to nineteen—become pregnant. The rate of teen pregnancy in the United States is more than twice as high as that in any other developed country and nearly ten times that in Japan or the Netherlands. The babies of these teens have an increased risk of premature birth, low birth weight, early infant death, and mental retardation. Teen mothers themselves are more likely than adult mothers to suffer from pregnancy-related health problems and sexually transmitted diseases (STDs).

Teen Pregnancy and Single Parenthood

If this situation sounds bad, consider also that the problem of teen pregnancy in America grows worse with each year. Although the overall rate of teen pregnancy decreased slightly during the 1990s, the rate of pregnancy among *unmarried* teens skyrocketed during the last half of the twentieth century—and continues to rise. During the 1950s and 1960s, a greater overall percentage of teens was becoming pregnant, but most teenage births were to married parents. Today, the opposite is true. *Adoptive Families* journal reports that the percentage of teen mothers aged fifteen to seventeen who were unmarried "more than tripled between 1950 and 1996, rising from 23 percent to 84 percent."[1] Among teen mothers aged eighteen and nineteen, those who were unmarried numbered 71 percent in 1996—almost eight times the percentage in 1950. Ninety-seven percent of all teen births in Washington, D.C., are to unmarried mothers.

So many teen mothers are unmarried that teen pregnancy has become a crisis for society as a whole. Single parenthood itself causes a large number of problems, the most devastating of which is poverty. According to a study conducted by the Robin Hood Foundation, "80 percent of . . . young, single mothers will live below the poverty line."[2] Most of the remaining 20 percent live on the edge of poverty. As Barbara Dafoe Whitehead writes, "For the vast majority of single mothers, the economic spectrum turns out to be narrow, running between precarious and desperate."[3]

But single mothers who have their first baby during adolescence are even worse off. Minimally educated and inexperienced in the workplace, teenagers are ill equipped to succeed

in a competitive job market. Their low earning potential, combined with the exorbitant costs of raising a child, make it nearly impossible for teen mothers ever to reach financial security.

The Children of Teen Mothers

Single teen mothers who are unable to support themselves and their children impose serious financial burdens on society: Over $19 billion in public funds is spent each year on antipoverty programs, health care, and nutrition to support families started by teenagers. However, it is the children of single teen mothers who pay the true costs of teen pregnancy. Patrick F. Fagan, a scholar of family and culture studies, explains why poverty and single parenthood make a dangerous combination for children:

> With both the single parent family background and the poverty that accompanies it . . . children [of teen mothers] will be twice as likely to drop out of high school . . . and be 1.4 times as likely to be out of school and unemployed. They will miss more schooldays, have lower education aspirations, get lower grades, and will divorce more as adults. They will be twice as likely to exhibit anti-social behavior as adults and be a quarter to 50 percent more likely to manifest behavioral problems such as anxiety, depression, hyperactivity, or dependence, and be two to three times more likely to need psychiatric care, or to commit suicide as teenagers.[4]

These problems occur in part because teenage mothers do not have the experience or maturity to be successful parents. As columnist Kathryn Simpson notes, the children of teen mothers "have the disadvantage of being cared for by someone who obviously hasn't lived enough to have coping skills, problem-solving ability or even common sense."[5] Consequently, teen mothers are more likely than adult parents to neglect or even abuse their children. A study conducted by Robert M. George and Bong Joo Lee discovered that "by age 5, on average, children born to age 17 or younger mothers were about one and one-half times more likely to become victims of . . . child abuse and neglect than were children born to 20- to 21-year-old mothers."[6]

Tomorrow's Criminals

The problems that plague the children of teen mothers do not simply fade away with time. These children usually grow up to be troubled adults, prone to drug addiction, depression, and violent or antisocial behavior. Not surprisingly, a large proportion of them become criminals. The male children of teen mothers are more than two and a half times more likely than children of older mothers to end up in jail. One study estimates that "70% of the prisoners in the United States [are] the children of teen mothers."[7]

Therefore, teen motherhood contributes enormously to society's rising crime rate, as well as to the costs associated with crime, such as law enforcement and other criminal justice expenses. Researcher Jeffrey Grogger states that if only teen mothers were to postpone childbearing until the age of twenty-three, "their sons' incarceration risk would fall by 17 percent . . . and corrections costs incurred by local, state, and federal governments would decrease by $1.29 billion per year."[8]

The Devastating Cycles of Teen Motherhood

Despite the clear link between teen motherhood and crime, many people claim that teen motherhood is an individual choice and should not be condemned. This view, however, contradicts the mounting evidence that teen motherhood contributes to society's largest problems. As Suzanne Fields writes, "the increasing numbers of children born to children are likely to repeat the devastating cycles of almost everything bad—teen-age pregnancy, school failure, early behavioral problems, drug abuse, child abuse, depression and crime."[9]

And, since the female children of teen mothers are two and a half times as likely as others to become single teen mothers themselves, these cycles promise to endure until society makes a concentrated effort to break them.

1. *Adoptive Families*, November/December 1998, p. 6.

2. Quoted in Joe S. McIlhaney Jr., "Q: Are Abstinence-Only Sex-Education Programs Good for Children? Yes: 'Safe-Sex' Education Has Failed. It's Time to Give Kids the Good News About Abstinence," *Insight*, September 29, 1997, p. 24.

3. Barbara Dafoe Whitehead, "Dan Quayle Was Right," *Atlantic Monthly*, April 1993.

4. Patrick F. Fagan, "Out of Wedlock Pregnancy: Derailing the Future Generation." Testimony before the House Subcommittee on Empowerment, July 16, 1998.

5. Kathryn Simpson, "Teen Pregnancy Affects All of Us: Young Moms Unready for Life's Stresses," *Arizona Republic*, January 13, 1999, p. 2.

6. Robert M. George and Bong Joo Lee, in Rebecca A. Maynard, ed., *Kids Having Kids: Economic Costs and Social Consequences of Teen Pregnancy*. Washington, DC: Urban Institute Press, 1997, p. 210.

7. *Education Digest*, "Curricular Programs to Curb Teen Pregnancy," March 1999, p. 38.

8. Jeffrey Grogger, in Maynard, ed., *Kids Having Kids*, p. 252.

9. Suzanne Fields, "The Crime of Children Having Children," *Washington Times*, April 15, 1996, in Stephen P. Thompson, ed., *Teen Pregnancy: Opposing Viewpoints*. San Diego: Greenhaven Press, 1997, p. 18.

"There was never an 'epidemic' of teen pregnancy."

The Problem of Teen Pregnancy Is Exaggerated

By every indication, the problem of teen pregnancy is improving. According to a 1998 study conducted by the National Center of Health Statistics (NCHS), the number of teenagers giving birth fell 16 percent between the years 1991 and 1997. A 1999 report by the Alan Guttmacher Institute states that teen pregnancy rates have decreased 17 percent during the 1990s—and today stand at the lowest level since 1973.

The declines hold true across all ethnic and racial groups in America. Citing statistics published by the NCHS, Pat Wingert writes:

> The pregnancy rate among African-American teens— traditionally higher than those of whites—is down by an even greater amount [than the decline in national rates]: 21 percent since 1991, the lowest level ever reported. The report also shows that the teen-pregnancy rate among Hispanics, though still the highest in the nation, tumbled 4.8 percent between 1995 and 1996.[1]

Never an Epidemic
The media has made much of the decline in teen pregnancy and birth rates, heralding it as the first good news about teen

pregnancy in ages. However, the truth of the matter is that teen pregnancy was never a drastic problem to begin with—and was certainly never the "epidemic" the media portrayed it to be. Douglas Kirby, in his comprehensive study of teen sexual behavior published in the *Journal of School Health*, writes that "There was never an 'epidemic' of teen pregnancy. The word, epidemic, suggests something that is rapidly increasing. In fact, the teen pregnancy rate was much lower in the 1970s, 1980s and 1990s, than it was in the 1950s."[2] In fact, a far smaller percentage of teens are becoming pregnant today than in the past. As Molly Ivins writes, "Both the rate of teen pregnancy and the total numbers [of pregnant teens] are dropping—and have been for 40 years."[3]

"The Single Most Important Social Problem of Our Time"

If teen pregnancy has been declining since the 1950s, why has the issue produced so much hysteria in recent years? The false impression that teen pregnancy is a growing problem was generated by political conservatives and exacerbated by irresponsible media reporting. Charles Murray, one influential conservative writer, contributed heavily to the national fervor over teen pregnancy. In a 1993 article for the *Wall Street Journal*, Murray condemned out-of-wedlock births by teens and adult women as "the single most important social problem of our time—more important than crime, drugs, poverty, illiteracy, welfare or homelessness."[4]

Without bothering to analyze whether out-of-wedlock births really did cause these problems, the media promoted Murray's thesis with its own unsubstantiated statements. *Newsweek* alleged that out-of-wedlock teen pregnancy was "the smoking gun in a sickening array of pathologies—crime, drug abuse, physical and mental illness, and welfare dependency."[5] *USA Today* wrote, "Beyond the drugs and the gunfire lies what is perhaps the most shocking of social pathologies: rates of out-of-wedlock births."[6]

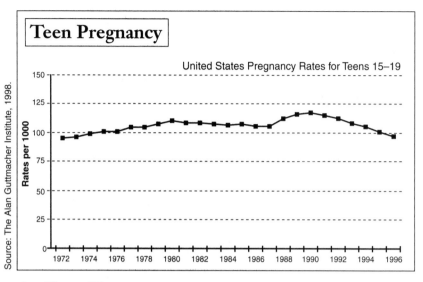

Source: The Alan Guttmacher Institute, 1998.

An Easy Target

The notion that out-of-wedlock births have such a grave impact on America's social problems has never been supported by statistical research. However, unmarried teen mothers make a useful scapegoat for every problem from "decaying morals" to rising rates of crime. Social commentator Sue Woodman explains why society is eager to cast blame on teen mothers:

> Pregnant teens are an easy target: they are a young, impoverished, and largely disenfranchised segment of the U.S. public. Because it involves poor, mostly unmarried young mothers, the teen pregnancy issue taps into a vengeful national mood that . . . demands harsh, ideological solutions to complex and seemingly intractable problems.[7]

In a society that is highly moralistic and self-righteous, it is easier for politicians to condemn teen mothers for their "bad behavior" than to tackle the larger problems that cause teen pregnancy, such as poverty, sexual abuse, and a hypersexualized media. As Woodman writes, "To face the issue of teen pregnancy head-on, politicians would have to assume the unpopular stance of protecting rather than punishing. The agenda should not be to blame girls but to fight against sexual predators, violence and incest at home, and a merchandising ethos that capitalizes on sex."[8]

Teen Pregnancy and the Welfare Debate

However, instead of approaching the problem of teenage pregnancy with honesty and compassion, politicians prefer to use the issue as a political tool. Conservatives have had a special reason for promoting hysteria over teen pregnancy: welfare. In order to gain political support for their goal to end welfare, conservatives painted out-of-wedlock mothers in a negative light, casting them either as manipulators scamming the welfare system or as promiscuous "baby machines." Due in part to these tactics, conservatives were able to gain bipartisan support for their goal to end welfare. As of 1996, welfare reform measures severely restricted welfare benefits to all single mothers and their children, and made teenage mothers virtually ineligible for government support.

Such measures are unlikely to make an impact on teen pregnancy—since teenagers certainly do not have babies just to get welfare checks—but they do promote negative stereotypes about teen mothers. Today, such stereotypes are so ingrained that teen mothers are automatically viewed as terrible burdens on society. New research, however, is finally challenging this view. According to Kirby, some recent studies confirm that "teen childbearing [has] remarkably little long-term impact on either the teen mothers or fathers."[9]

Society should help prevent teenagers from becoming pregnant before they are ready, but it should not demonize those teens who do have children. If society truly wants to help teen mothers raise their children successfully, it must offer protection, not punishment.

---

1. Pat Wingert, "The Battle Over Falling Birth Rates," *Newsweek*, May 11, 1998, p. 40.

2. Douglas Kirby, "Reflections on Two Decades of Research on Teen Sexual Behavior and Pregnancy," *Journal of School Health*, March 1999, p. 98.

3. Molly Ivins, "Teen Mothers Lack Good Role Models," *Liberal Opinion Week*, September 22, 1997, p. 12.

4. Charles Murray, "The Coming White Underclass," *Wall Street Journal*, October 29, 1993.

5. Quoted in Janine Jackson, "The 'Crisis' of Teen Pregnancy: Girls Pay the Price for Media Distortion," *Extra!* March/April 1994.

6. Quoted in Jackson, "The 'Crisis' of Teen Pregnancy."

7. Sue Woodman, "How Teen Pregnancy Has Become a Political Football," *Ms.*, January/February 1995.

8. Woodman, "How Teen Pregnancy Has Become a Political Football."

9. Kirby, "Reflections on Two Decades of Research on Teen Sexual Behavior," p. 98.

"Most teen mothers raise their children single-handedly—a task that is difficult even for mature, financially stable women."

Pregnancy Harms Teens' Lives

This is what three teenage girls have to say about being parents:

- I'm not living with my family. I'm living with a friend. It's really bleak and confusing. I miss everything I left behind.

- If I thought I didn't have freedom before the baby, I didn't know what freedom was. My parents watch every step I take. After all, they are paying for me and my baby.

- After they cut Marquis's umbilical cord, they just put him up on me and I told 'em, "Get that ugly baby off me!" . . . I didn't want to accept that at fifteen I have a baby.[1]

These teenage girls, who are too young to even contemplate their next semester in school, have suddenly found themselves faced with the greatest responsibility of life: raising another human being. It is a responsibility that will alter their lives forever. Even in the best of circumstances, teens who become pregnant face long-term consequences. *Kids Having Kids*, a 1996 report on teenage pregnancy, "reveals that only 30 percent of girls who become pregnant before age 18 will earn a high-school diploma by the age of 30."[2] In addition, columnist Joe S. McIlhaney Jr. reports that "adolescent dads . . . do not progress as far educationally and earn, on average, about $2,000 less annually at age 27 as a direct result of the impact of teen parenthood."[3]

Facing Parenthood Alone

If the long-term consequences of teen pregnancy are bad, the short-term can be even worse. At a time when they are in greatest need of love and support, most pregnant teens find themselves alone. Boyfriends who seemed caring and devoted suddenly disappear from the scene. Like many pregnant teens, Robyn was abandoned by her boyfriend when she told him she was pregnant:

> I dated John for about a year. He always told me that if anything happened he would take care of me. When I told him I was pregnant he said that it wasn't his baby. He dropped me and started dating my best friend. It was hard for me to accept that he didn't care as much as he said he did before I got pregnant.[4]

In fact, 80 percent of pregnant teens do not marry the fathers of their children. Nor do teen fathers offer much in the way of financial or emotional support. One study found that fewer than 10 percent of teen fathers visit their children more than once a week.

The Struggle of Single Motherhood

Therefore, most teen mothers raise their children single-handedly—a task that is difficult even for mature, financially stable women. Unlike most adult mothers, however, teen mothers usually suffer from severe financial troubles. Those who are not fortunate enough to have the financial support of their own parents must rely on desperate measures. Many work two or even three jobs to afford the expense of daycare,

A pregnant teen risks alienation from family and friends at a time when she sorely needs their support.

health insurance for their child, and other child-related costs. Some teens sleep with their infants on the floors of friends' homes. A significant minority ends up in emergency shelters or even on the streets.

Welfare used to protect teen mothers and their children from destitution and homelessness. However, recent reforms in welfare law require that teen mothers live with their parents and attend high school to be eligible for welfare. Those who do receive welfare often live in poverty due to dwindling benefits.

An Unpleasant Responsibility

Those teenage parents who do have adequate financial resources, usually because of the generosity of their own parents, also have difficult lives. Parenthood is an arduous, tedious, and often unpleasant responsibility. It involves changing dirty diapers every two hours, getting up again and again in the middle of the night to calm a crying baby, trying to function at work or at school without sleep, and having no free time to see friends or even to sleep in on the weekends. As one teen parent sums up, "It's really, really hard. I've got to get up with him during the night, then get up early for school. . . . In the evening, I've got to do my homework, feed him, give him a bath, get him to sleep and get myself ready for the next day."[5]

Many teen mothers have an idealized view of pregnancy and believe that the love and companionship they will receive from their baby will compensate for the hardship of being a teen parent. However, babies are simply unable to provide their mothers with emotional support or even love. As Kaplan writes, "Babies need far more love from their mothers than they can give. Teen mothers experience bitter disappointment when they do not receive the love they expect from their babies. Motherhood puts tremendous demands upon the mothers' time, energy, and emotions, demands for which they are not prepared."[6]

Missing Out on Childhood

Teenagers are not prepared for the demands of parenthood simply because they are still children. This is why pregnancy at a young age is such a tragedy. Parenthood catapults teens instantly into adulthood, robbing them of the joys of being a child. Once these opportunities are missed, they are gone for good. As one teen mother says, "I've missed out on a lot of teenage things like dances, parties, or just having fun. I have three jobs now, and spend most of my money on food, diapers, and child needs. . . . To all teens thinking about having sex, don't make the same mistake I did."[7] Another says, "I feel like I'm 40 years old. I missed out on my whole childhood."[8]

Teenagers should be going to parties, playing sports, and dreaming about their futures—not changing diapers. Most teen parents would give anything to have the carefree lifestyle of an ordinary teen, but unfortunately, they can never turn back.

1. Elaine Bell Kaplan, *Not Our Kind of Girl: Unraveling the Myths of Black Teenage Motherhood.* Los Angeles: University of California Press, 1997, p. 184.

2. Quoted in Joe S. McIlhaney Jr., "Q: Are Abstinence-Only Sex-Education Programs Good for Children? Yes: 'Safe Sex' Education Has Failed. It's Time to Give Kids the Good News About Abstinence," *Insight*, September 29, 1997, p. 24.

3. Joe S. McIlhaney Jr., "Q: Are Abstinence-Only Sex-Education Programs Good for Children?" p. 24.

4. Kristin Luker, *Dubious Conceptions: The Politics of Teen Pregnancy.* Cambridge, MA: Harvard University Press, 1996, p. 151.

5. Quoted in National Campaign to Prevent Teen Pregnancy, "Teens Comment On," p. 1. On-line. Internet. Available http://www.teenpregnancy.org/teen/teenrent.htm.

6. Kaplan, *Not Our Kind of Girl,* p. 184.

7. Quoted in National Campaign to Prevent Teen Pregnancy, "Teens Comment On," p. 1.

8. Quoted in National Campaign to Prevent Teen Pregnancy, "Teens Comment On," p. 2

"Instead of limiting their opportunities, parenthood actually motivates many teens to work harder and to expect more from their lives than they would have otherwise."

Pregnancy Improves Some Teens' Lives

Virtually every discussion of teen pregnancy relies on the same implicit assumption: Pregnancy ruins teens' lives. From the way the issue is portrayed by the media, one would think that pregnancy consigned teens to lives of misery, destitution, and regret.

The experience of Angie Hernandez, a teen mother residing in Tampa Bay, Florida, however, belies this view. At seventeen, she lives happily with her baby Anthony and her husband Joshua, the baby's father. She is working toward her equivalency diploma and plans to attend college. "I don't miss anything from my old life," she says. "I'm glad this happened."[1]

A surprisingly large number of teen parents say the same thing. One teenage girl declares that the times spent with her infant have been "the best of her life."[2] A young man who was involved in drugs and crime before his girlfriend became pregnant states, "I like being a father and having a family. It's a challenge."[3]

Meeting the Challenge of Parenthood

Most adults assume that parenthood "ruins" teens' lives by burdening them with responsibility at too young an age. In reality, many teens find that the challenge of parenthood vastly *improves* their lives. Instead of limiting their opportunities, parenthood actually motivates many teens to work harder and to expect more from their lives than they would have otherwise. As Terry Parks, an eighteen-year-old with a two-year-old son, explains, "My child . . . gives me a reason to keep going and to strive for more. . . . The thought that he's there, too, is what really gives me that push to do more for myself. He's a good boy. He's saved my life in a lot of ways."[4]

Dana Little, who became pregnant at age fifteen, makes a similar comment about her son: "He gives me a push, makes me strive to do better. . . . He's been very positive in my life."[5]

In many cases, the desire to be a good parent acts as a powerful incentive for young people to abandon a destructive lifestyle—one that involves drinking, drug abuse, or promiscuous sex, for example—in favor of a responsible one. Many teens who had performed poorly in school before their preg-

Highly focused and motivated teens may find some aspects of parenthood rewarding.

nancies become focused on educational and career goals after having a baby. Scholar Kristin Luker writes that

> Some young women say [that having a child] was the best thing they ever did. In a few cases it leads to marriage or a stable relationship; in many others it motivates a woman to push herself for her baby's sake; and in still other cases it enhances the woman's self-esteem, since it enables her to do something productive, something nurturing and socially responsible.[6]

For Some, a Way Out

Moreover, for the thousands of teens who suffer abuse each year, pregnancy is one of the few means of escape from their abusers. In fact, a large proportion of teenage girls who become pregnant live in troubled homes or experience sexual, physical, or emotional abuse at the hands of family members. Sociologist Mike Males reports that

> [A] study of pregnant teens and teenaged mothers showed that two-thirds had been raped or sexually abused, nearly always by parents, other guardians, or relatives. Six in ten teen mothers' childhoods also included severe physical violence: being beaten with a stick, strap, or fist, thrown against walls, deprived of food, locked in closets, or burned with cigarettes or hot water.[7]

Many abused teens find that pregnancy gives them an opportunity to improve their situation. Pregnancy often motivates these teens to leave home so as not to subject their new babies to an abusive home life. Some end up at emergency shelters for pregnant mothers, where they stay until they complete school and find a stable living situation. Yale Gancherov, a supervising social worker at the Crittenton Center for Young Women in Los Angeles, contends that the teen mothers who reside at the center are better off than they were before they became pregnant: "The parents of these young women were violent, were drug abusers, were sexually abusive, were absent or neglectful. While privileged people may see a detriment in a teenager becoming a mother, these girls see it as a realistic improvement in their lives."[8]

Almonica, a sixteen-year-old pregnant teen, came to the Crittenton Center having recently witnessed her stepfather burn her mother to death during a drunken fight. Almonica says that getting pregnant was her "way out"[9] of what could be a similar fate.

Not a Tragedy

Cases like Almonica's, in which teen pregnancy was a positive step, are rarely mentioned because they do not send the "appropriate" message to teens about teen pregnancy. However, it is wrong to misrepresent the effects of teen pregnancy, even for the purpose of discouraging teens from parenthood. Although pregnancy is certainly not the best choice for most teens, it is also not the tragedy that it is made out to be. Society should stop demonizing teen parents and instead recognize them as human beings struggling to meet the challenges life brings them—and often doing so successfully and happily.

1. Quoted in Fawn Germer, "Babies Are Grown-Up Reality," *Tampa Tribune*, December 13, 1998, p. 1.

2. Quoted in Germer, "Babies Are Grown-Up Reality," p. 1.

3. Quoted in Germer, "Babies Are Grown-Up Reality," p. 1.

4. Quoted in Elaine Bell Kaplan, *Not Our Kind of Girl: Unraveling the Myths of Black Teenage Motherhood*. Los Angeles: University of California Press, 1997, p. 122.

5. Quoted in Kaplan, *Not Our Kind of Girl*, p. 122.

6. Kristin Luker, *Dubious Conceptions: The Politics of Teen Pregnancy*. Cambridge, MA: Harvard University Press, 1996, p. 182.

7. Mike Males, "In Defense of Teenaged Mothers," *Progressive*, August 1994, p. 22.

8. Males, "In Defense of Teenaged Mothers," p. 22.

9. Douglas Kirby, "Reflections on Two Decades of Research on Teen Sexual Behavior and Pregnancy," *Journal of School Health*, March 1999, p. 89.

CHAPTER 2

What Factors Contribute to Teen Pregnancy?

"Eighty percent of unwed teenage mothers . . . were raised in an environment of extreme poverty."

Poverty Is a Factor in Teen Pregnancy

When asked by an interviewer what she had dreamed of before she had become a teen mother, Shanika, a twenty-four-year-old with three kids, no high school degree, and no job, replied, "You know, I really didn't have a dream."[1]

Shanika is among the 80 percent of unwed teenage mothers who were raised in an environment of extreme poverty. Many of these poor teen mothers grew up lacking even basic resources such as health care, adequate nutrition, and safe homes. Kristin Luker, author of *Dubious Conceptions: The Politics of Teen Pregnancy*, describes the kind of life teen mothers like Shanika have experienced:

> They were born poor and grew up in poor neighborhoods. Their early lives were often scarred by violence and disorder, including sexual abuse. They attended rundown, underequipped schools in which teachers struggled to discipline and motivate the students, and they were typically not among the lucky and clever few who managed to obtain a little extra attention from their teachers, coaches, or adult neighbors. They were born into families that were at the end of the social and economic queue, and their life experiences rarely moved them any closer to the front.[2]

It is not difficult to understand, then, why Shanika did not have childhood dreams for the future. Poor teens often believe that they have little chance of escaping the communities where they were raised. Unfortunately, their feelings of hopelessness are not without basis. As Luker explains:

> The odds against achieving even . . . modest dreams are getting longer. Young women with limited educational and labor market skills face many more obstacles to a stable relationship and a secure job than they used to, especially when they are members of minority groups and come from poor homes. And the young men in their lives have bleaker employment prospects than ever, making them a slender reed for young women to rely upon.[3]

Using Sex as an Escape

The feelings of hopelessness so prevalent in poor communities help explain why so many teens from poor backgrounds

Teens often experience feelings of hopelessness; engaging in sex can provide an escape from their problems.

become parents before they are ready. As Michael A. Carrera, a scholar on teen sexuality, theorizes, many poor teens may engage in sex as a way to temporarily escape the problems and stresses of their lives. He writes that

> Most [poor] young people see little employment op-portunity around them and will probably face a life of low economic status, ever-present racism, and inade-quate opportunities for quality education. . . . Growing numbers of adolescent voices are now saying, "There is no hope. There is no one who values me. There is no one who cares." Under such conditions, it is no wonder that some young people, instead of becoming industrious and hopeful, become sexually intimate for a short-term sense of comfort. . . . In such cases, inter-course is used as a coping mechanism.[4]

Scholars Robert Cole and Geoffrey Stokes also conclude from their research that many disadvantaged teens turn to sex as a reprieve from "a life that can be, often enough, boring or demanding or puzzling."[5]

An Act of Hope

Many poor teens who are sexually active lack access to birth control—or have access but cannot afford the expense. Schools in their communities are far less likely than other schools to provide sex-education courses. However, even those poor teens who do have adequate knowledge about and access to contraception may not be sufficiently motivated to avoid pregnancy.

Unlike middle-class teenage girls, poor teenage girls do not have the promise of college or a career as an incentive to post-pone early pregnancy. In fact, many regard motherhood as the only role available to them—and the only role in which they feel they might succeed. Therefore, for many teen mothers who live in poverty, having a child is an act of hope, because it offers them—or at least their children—a chance for a better life. As Luker writes, "Having a baby is a lottery ticket for many teenagers: it brings with it at least the dream of something better, and if the dream fails, not much is lost."[6]

Just as poor teenage girls sometimes turn to motherhood as a chance to improve their lives, some poor teenage boys view fatherhood as an emblem of pride or a way to add meaning to their existence. For example, community worker John Williams states that in some gang communities, "Many of these people don't think they'll live a long time, so having a child is their way of expressing themselves, of proving they have relevance."[7] One former Los Angeles gang member, Osvaldo Cruz, whose teenage girlfriend's pregnancy was not accidental, says that "there was an emptiness inside of me, and I thought if I have a baby, I could give him everything I couldn't have."[8]

Never a Good Time to Have Kids

The current debate about teen pregnancy, by failing to address why many teens may choose to have babies, betrays a lack of understanding of the difficulties faced by the poor. Most Americans contend that teenagers would be better off if they waited to have children until they reached adulthood and became financially secure. What this argument fails to acknowledge, however, is that the majority of the poor never reach financial security. As well-paying industrial jobs are replaced by low-wage jobs in the service industry due to changes in the American economy, poor people are increasingly unable to afford parenthood. As Luker explains, "Given the scarcity of decent jobs, a substantial minority of Americans simply cannot afford to have children. . . . A child born to married parents who can fully support it is, like safe neighborhoods and good schools, becoming a luxury accessible only to the wealthy."[9] A poor teen who postpones having a baby until adulthood, then, is not significantly better off than a poor teen who does not—which means that poor teens have little reason to prevent pregnancy.

Consequently, the most effective way to deal with the issue of teen pregnancy is to expand opportunities for the poor, so that disadvantaged teens feel they have other options besides parenthood, and so that girls like Shanika have the luxury of dreaming.

1. Quoted in Molly Ivins, "Teen Mothers Lack Good Role Models," *Liberal Opinion Week*, September 22, 1997, p. 12.

2. Kristin Luker, *Dubious Conceptions: The Politics of Teen Pregnancy*. Cambridge, MA: Harvard University Press, 1996, p. 180.

3. Luker, *Dubious Conceptions*, p. 137.

4. Michael A. Carrera, "Preventing Adolescent Pregnancy: In Hot Pursuit," *Siecus Report*, August/September 1995, p. 16.

5. Quoted in Elaine Bell Kaplan, *Not Our Kind of Girl: Unraveling the Myths of Black Teenage Motherhood*. Los Angeles: University of California Press, 1997, p. 41.

6. Luker, *Dubious Conceptions*, p. 182.

7. Quoted in Sarah Yang, "Teen Pregnancy Programs Begin to Target Males," *Los Angeles Times*, June 24, 1999, p. B1.

8. Quoted in Yang, "Teen Pregnancy Programs Begin to Target Males," p. B1.

9. Luker, *Dubious Conceptions*, p. 179.

"Most pregnant teens have one thing in common: They lack adequate support and supervision from their parents."

Lack of Parental Guidance Contributes to Teen Pregnancy

One teenager sums up the problem of teen pregnancy in this way:

> I think a lot of teens don't feel connected with their parents. They don't have the family structures. They are sort of by themselves. They rely more on their friends for support. And once you start relying on your friends, the judgment that your parents would usually have and that structure aren't necessarily there.[1]

This insightful comment cuts to the heart of the problem of teen pregnancy. Teens become pregnant due to a variety of factors, but most pregnant teens have one thing in common: They lack adequate support and supervision from their parents.

Lack of Supervision

In this day and age, when American adults work anywhere from forty to seventy hours a week, lack of parental supervision has become the norm. Teenagers are typically without adult supervision for at least three hours a day. The consequences of this should be obvious. During the unsupervised after-school hours, teenagers tend to get in trouble with the law, experiment with drugs and alcohol—and have sex. In one study of 1,228 parochial-school students, three out of four sexually experienced teenagers reported first having sex in an unsupervised home. Kristine Napier, author of *The Power of Abstinence*, contends that "the most common place for teens to have sex in is in the home after school when parents aren't there."[2]

Providing adequate supervision is difficult for most parents, but single parents are at a particular disadvantage. Single-parent families are more likely than two-parent families to suffer from poverty or financial worries, and as a result they tend to work long hours or hold down multiple jobs. As columnist Lisa Fernandez explains, "Hard-working parents, often running single-family households, do not have enough time for [their children], let alone [for] a discussion on sex."[3]

The lack of supervision in many single-parent families helps account for why the children of teen mothers are more than two and a half times as likely as other children to become teen parents themselves. Teen mothers are usually unmarried and poor, and most lack the education or skills necessary to improve their incomes. These factors, coupled with the extraordinary demands of being a parent at a young age, make it difficult for teen mothers to provide adequate supervision for their children. Susan, a teen mother whose mother had also been pregnant as a teen, said that it was easy for her to have sex because "[with] my mother, I knew . . . I could do anything I wanted. She wouldn't care."[4]

Communicating About Sex

Susan also reported that her mother had not offered her any information about sex. In fact, most teens who became pregnant had never discussed issues of sex or dating with their parents. Some pregnant teens demonstrate a shocking lack of knowledge about even basic aspects of sexuality. Elaine Bell Kaplan, who interviewed teenage mothers for her book *Not*

Our Kind of Girl: Unraveling the Myths of Black Teenage Mother-hood, writes that "most of the teenage mothers [surveyed] did not fully understand the menstrual cycle. . . . They did not make the connection between the start of menstruation and their ability to become pregnant."[5] Kaplan also states that many pregnant teens believed that they could not get pregnant the first time they had sex.

Why would parents fail to convey such essential information to their children? A large number are too busy or uncomfortable to talk about sex. Others fear that by broaching the issue of sex, they may be encouraging their children to have it.

More common, however, are parents who feel that the issue is "covered" if they just forbid their children to have sex. Pregnant teens often state that their mothers took this approach:

Only thing she said was, "Don't be out here messing with no boys." And that was it. . . .

I love my mother, but she never really talked to me, and I don't feel I can talk to her about private matters. She acts like we shouldn't talk about sex. She only told me after my period, that I shouldn't go with boys. . . .

She didn't want me to know nothing about sex but "just don't do it." But I was like— . . . gosh, but everybody is doing this and I wanted to try it, too.[6]

Other parents actually promote lies about sexuality, usually as a scare tactic to prevent their children from having sex. Hoping to discourage her daughter from having sex, the mother of pregnant sixteen-year-old Marnie Martin provided false information about birth control. Instead, she only made Marnie scared to use birth control: "I went to my mother and said, 'Well mom, I like this boy and I might be doing something with him and would you take me to get birth control?' And she said, 'No, because once you start taking those pills you'll become sterile.'"[7]

Parents Can Encourage Abstinence

Mothers such as Marnie's often believe that they must rely on scare tactics because they cannot convince their children to abstain from sex. Yet studies show that parents are the single most important influence on whether their kids have sex or become pregnant. Teens who discuss sex openly with their parents are less likely than other teens to become sexually active and more likely to use birth control if they do have sex. Linda Chavez, citing a two-decade research study by the National Campaign to Prevent Teen Pregnancy, writes that

Open communication about sex between parents and teens often leads to more responsible behavior by teens in the area of sexuality.

- Teens who are close to their parents are more likely to [be] abstinent, [or to] have fewer sexual partners and use contraceptives when they do become sexually active.

- Teens whose parents closely supervise them are more likely to be older when they first have sex and [overall] have fewer partners.[8]

Parents do have the power to prevent their children from becoming pregnant as teens. However, too many parents fail to supervise their teenagers or refuse to openly discuss their questions about sex. In order to solve problems such as teen pregnancy, parents need to take a stronger role in their children's lives. As commentator Linda Chavez writes, "We'd have a lot fewer new teen parents if adults would take their own responsibilities as parents more seriously."[9]

1. Quoted in the National Campaign to Prevent Teen Pregnancy, *What About the Teens? Research on What Teens Say About Teen Pregnancy: A Focus Group Report.* Washington, DC, 1999, p. 15.

2. Quoted in Cheryl Wetzstein, "Teaching Abstinence in Schools," *Insight,* September 22, 1997, p. 39.

3. Lisa Fernandez, "Cut Sought in Latina Teen Births," *San Francisco Chronicle,* February 9, 1999, p. A13.

4. Quoted in Elaine Bell Kaplan, *Not Our Kind of Girl: Unraveling the Myths of Black Teenage Motherhood.* Los Angeles: University of California Press, 1997, p. 34.

5. Kaplan, *Not Our Kind of Girl,* p. 38.

6. Quoted in Kristin Luker, *Dubious Conceptions: The Politics of Teen Pregnancy.* Cambridge, MA: Harvard University Press, 1996, p. 140.

7. Kaplan, *Not Our Kind of Girl,* p. 39.

8. Quoted in Linda Chavez, "Ironically, a Drop in Teen Sex Comes at a Time When Many Adults Have Given Up Trying to Preach Abstinence," *Enterprise/Salt Lake City,* February 15, 1999, p. 14.

9. Chavez, "Ironically, A Drop in Teen Sex," p. 14.

"Almost two-thirds of adolescent mothers have partners older than twenty years of age."

Adult Men Are Largely to Blame for Teen Pregnancy

Most of the measures society takes to reduce teenage pregnancy are aimed at convincing teens to abstain from sex or promoting the reliable use of birth control. The underlying assumption of such measures is that if teenagers would just act more responsibly, most cases of adolescent pregnancy could be prevented.

However, focusing on teen behavior does nothing to eliminate the primary cause of teenage pregnancy: the exploitation of adolescent girls by adult men. Take the case of twenty-nine-year-old Tyrone Gaskins, who was "dating" a twelve-year-old teen for several months before she became pregnant. Should society really fault the young girl—and not the grown man who took advantage of her—for this unwanted pregnancy? Yet in all too many cases, it is the girls who take the blame and bear the consequences when they are impregnated by adult men.

A Widespread Problem

While the case of Gaskins obviously represents the extreme, the problem of adult men impregnating teenage girls is hardly uncommon. In fact, the results of two recent studies show that the vast majority of teen pregnancies are fathered by adults—not by "adult" eighteen-year-old high school students, but by men who are out of school and usually over the age of twenty. According to a 1995 study published in *Family Planning Perspectives,* almost two-thirds of adolescent mothers have partners older than twenty years of age. Furthermore, a 1998 report conducted by sociologist Mike Males concludes that "three fourths of the fathers in births . . . among . . . students [aged sixteen to eighteen] are postschool men."[1]

The trends among younger teens are especially disturbing. Research suggests that the younger the adolescent mother, the greater the age gap between her and her partner, with one study revealing that "fathers are on average 9.8 years older than mothers 11 to 12 years of age [and] 4.6 years older than mothers 13 to 14 years of age."[2]

Rape, Pure and Simple

These statistics offer a glimpse of the sickening reality behind so-called teen pregnancy. When a twenty-one-year-old man has sex with a twelve-year-old girl—or even a seventeen-year-old girl—it is rape, pure and simple. It doesn't matter whether the girl says she wanted to. Statutory rape laws forbid even consensual sex between adults and minors as a way to protect children and adolescents from sexual exploitation. And, as columnist Leonard Pitts Jr. writes, "Who ever needed protection more than a teen-age girl who is, or thinks she is, in love? Who was ever more vulnerable to exploitation by an older man willing to whisper the proper promises and tell the necessary lies?"[3]

Just as a sexual relationship between an adult and a child is always exploitative, so is a sexual relationship between an adult and a teenage girl. Teenage girls may be physically mature, but they are still children, and possess a child's need for love and acceptance. Their youth and inexperience make them particularly vulnerable to older men who are looking for sex. Patricia, who first had sex at age fourteen with a twenty-one-year-old man, explains why: "They know more than you," she says. "If I'm going out with a 25-year-old guy, what can I offer him that he hasn't already had? I'm just learning the rules. I have to show him that I can give him more."[4]

Sexual Abuse

Even more alarming than these supposedly consensual relationships between adult men and teenage girls are those that are outright abusive. The problem of sexual abuse among teens who become pregnant is widespread, but barely acknowledged. However, a shocking 66 percent of pregnant teens have histories of sexual abuse—most perpetrated by adult family members or older boyfriends.

Sexual abuse makes teens prone to pregnancy for a variety of reasons. First, pregnancy may be the direct result of an episode of abuse. In a study of 455 teen mothers, researcher H.P. Gershenson found that "over 60% had . . . coercive sexual experiences and 23% became pregnant by the perpetrator."[5]

Second, the trauma of sexual abuse makes teenage girls more likely to engage in the types of behavior that increase their chances of an unplanned pregnancy. As Elders writes,

> A history of sexual abuse has been linked to high-risk behaviors that may account for increased risk of early unplanned pregnancy, including young age at initiation of sexual intercourse, failure to use contraception, prostitution, physically assaultive relationships, and abuse of alcohol and other drugs. Moreover, girls with histories of sexual abuse have been found to have a greater desire to conceive and increased concerns about infertility than girls without abuse histories.[6]

Prosecuting Statutory Rapists

Some states are finally beginning to address the abusive relationships behind so many cases of teenage pregnancy. In California, officials have instituted aggressive efforts to prosecute and imprison adult men who have sex with minors. Since its inception in 1995, California's Statutory Rape Vertical Prosecution Program has convicted more than 1,454 offenders and has 5,000 more under investigation.

Other states must follow California's lead and treat statutory rapists as what they are: criminals. If older men know that they will suffer severe consequences for breaking statutory rape laws, perhaps they will think twice about taking advantage of young girls.

1. Mike Males, "Adult Partners and Adult Contexts of 'Teenage Sex,'" *Education and Urban Society*, February 1998, p. 189.

2. Joycelyn Elders, "Adolescent Pregnancy and Sexual Abuse," *Journal of the American Medical Association*, August 19, 1998, p. 648.

3. Leonard Pitts Jr., "It's Time for Older Men Who Impregnate Girls to Grow Up," *Houston Chronicle*, March 5, 1999, p. 2.

4. Quoted in Sarah Yang, "Teen Pregnancy Programs Begin to Target Males," *Los Angeles Times*, June 4, 1999, p. B1.

5. Quoted in Elders, "Adolescent Pregnancy and Sexual Abuse," p. 648.

6. Elders, "Adolescent Pregnancy and Sexual Abuse," p. 648.

"Teenage girls feel they must have sex in order to 'fit in,'
but at the same time, they face societal stigma for
appearing too interested in sex."

The Glamorization of Sex in Popular Culture Contributes to Teen Pregnancy

In today's society, most—if not all—teenagers are confronted with the decision of whether or not to have sex. Although individual values and parental expectations play a role in this decision, so do societal pressures. Teenage girls face a disproportionate amount of these pressures. Not only do they bear more of the consequences of early sexual involvement, but they are also immersed in a culture that makes it difficult for them to resist sexual involvement or to take initiative in using contraception. As Barbara Ehrenreich writes,

> A brave-enough girl can chart her own course through the sexual and reproductive perils of youth. She can say no to sex, despite the fact that sex is often the ticket to popularity and the prom. Or she can yes to sex and embrace it in a responsible, womanly way—by, for example, going out and getting a prescription for the Pill. . . . But, . . . we do not have a culture that fosters courage—or other positive, self-affirming traits—in its teenage girls.[1]

The Media and Sex

The primary message society sends teenage girls—and people in general—is that the world revolves around sex. Today's popular culture emphasizes this at every turn: Hollywood movies portray two strangers meeting, having sex, and then falling in love; MTV features sexual images of half-naked men and women; television sitcoms show young professionals joking about their one-night stands. As the media portrays it, everybody—especially the young and attractive—seems to be having sex.

Not surprisingly, popular culture's obsession with sex contributes to the pressure teens feel to have sex. This happens in two ways. First, certain television programs or movies make sex seem appealing by portraying it as glamorous, fun, and free of negative consequences. One teenager describes how this affects teens:

> I think the media can influence a lot of younger kids who don't know [about sex]. They think that [how sex is depicted on TV and in movies] is how it's going to be: You come home after the first date, you have sex with someone, and it's all glamorous, and that's it. They think because they see their favorite movie stars doing it, . . . they can just follow them.[2]

Second, the media shapes people's beliefs about what normal behavior is. Teenagers who are accustomed to seeing people have casual sex on television may believe that this type of behavior is normal—even expected. As one parent explains, "There's so many . . . general cultural and media messages that are so strong, so sexually potent, that I think that a lot of kids [are] getting the message that this is what's expected of them. Sex is expected. It's fun. They should be out there doing it."[3]

Girls and Advertising

While the media encourages all teens to have sex before they are ready, its influence on teenage girls is twofold. Unlike

Television bombards teens with both romantic and sexually charged images, which may encourage teens to become sexually active.

boys, teenage girls are the targets of an aggressive marketplace culture that uses images of sex and sexiness to sell products. In media advertising, sexiness—not intelligence or achievement—is portrayed as the most important characteristic a female can possess.

Moreover, the beauty and fashion advertising industry, with its endless array of self-improvement products and its glamorous images of thin models, sends the implicit message to teenage girls that they are not acceptable as they are. As social critics Barbara Dafoe Whitehead and Theodora Ooms write, "Distilled to its essence, the market message [to teenage girls] is: 'You are a mess.'"[4] Consequently, most teenage girls are preoccupied with their appearance and crave affirmation of their sexual attractiveness. Many of them feel pressured to have sex simply to prove to themselves and to others that they are desirable to males.

Contradictory Messages

Although the media actually promotes teenage sex, the rest of society sends the opposite message. The large majority of parents, religious leaders, and politicians believes that teens should refrain from sex, at least until they are legal adults.

Therefore, girls are faced with conflicting messages about how they should handle issues of sex. Teenage girls feel they must have sex in order to "fit in," but at the same time, they face societal stigma for appearing too interested in sex. As Kristin Luker writes, "On the one hand, young people are told 'just say no' [to sex]; on the other, their friends, the media, and society at large foster the idea that sexual activity among teenagers is widespread and increasingly commonplace."[5]

As a result, teenage girls may not want to seem "prepared" for sex by providing contraception. Luker writes that

> one simple way of showing that one is a "nice girl" is to be unprepared for sex—to have given no prior thought to contraception. . . . To use contraception, a woman has to anticipate sexual activity by locating the impetus within herself, rather than in the man who has overcome her hesitancy. She must plan for sex, must be prepared to speak about contraception frankly with someone she may not know very well . . . , and must put her own long-term welfare before the short-term pleasure of the couple, especially the man.[6]

In a society that frowns upon teenage girls having sex, it is unlikely that any but the most confident girls will take the initiative to prepare for a possible sexual encounter. This is why so many pregnant teens say that they didn't mean to get pregnant, "it just happened." Many teenage girls, in fact, do not decide on a course of action when it comes to sex; they merely go along with whatever their boyfriends suggest. This passivity is a reflection of the fact that teens have few support systems and role models if they want to abstain from sex.

If teenage girls are to reach adulthood before becoming pregnant, they need help and encouragement from society. One thing society can do is to challenge the values promoted by popular culture. Teenagers need to know that the media does not provide good lessons to live by.

1. Barbara Ehrenreich, "Where Have All the Babies Gone?" *Life*, January 1998, p. 68.

2. Quoted in the National Campaign to Prevent Teen Pregnancy, *What About the Teens? Research on What Teens Say About Teen Pregnancy: A Focus Group Report.* Washington, DC, 1999, p. 12.

3. Quoted in the National Campaign to Prevent Teen Pregnancy, *Where Are the Adults? A Focus Group Report.* Washington, DC, 1998, p. 23.

4. Barbara Dafoe Whitehead and Theodora Ooms, *Goodbye to Girlhood: What's Troubling Girls and What Can We Do About It?* Washington, DC: National Campaign to Prevent Pregnancy, 1999, p. 11.

5. Kristin Luker, *Dubious Conceptions: The Politics of Teen Pregnancy.* Cambridge, MA: Harvard University Press, 1996, p. 138.

6. Luker, *Dubious Conceptions*, p. 147.

CHAPTER 3

How Can Teen Pregnancy Be Prevented?

"Between the years 1991 and 1997, when the number of sexually active high school students fell 11 percent, teen pregnancy rates experienced an unprecedented decline of 16 percent."

Teaching Abstinence Reduces Teen Pregnancy

In 1993, the 15 million members of the Southern Baptist church announced "True Love Waits," their national campaign to challenge young people to refrain from sex until marriage. Defying even the most ambitious expectations, the effort has motivated more than 750,000 teens to sign commitment cards pledging to abstain from sex until marriage. Twenty years earlier, at the height of America's sexual revolution, the pro-virgin rallies held by True Love Waits would have inspired ridicule. Today, however, more and more teens are taking a serious look at abstinence. In fact, sexual abstinence is becoming so common among teenagers that *Marie Claire* magazine calls it "a new sexual revolution sweeping America—the biggest shift of social behavior since the free-love movement of the 1960s."[1] Some teenagers are choosing to abstain from sex for religious reasons, others because they fear AIDS or pregnancy, and still others because they know they are not ready for sex and its consequences.

Regardless of what motivates them to abstain from sex, abstinent teens sex share certain traits. They generally have higher levels of self-esteem and closer relationships with their parents than teens who have sex. They are less likely to be involved in drugs, alcohol, and other risky activities, and more likely to be goal-oriented.

A Powerful Weapon Against Teen Pregnancy

Beyond these benefits, the abstinence movement has also had a dramatic impact on preventing teen pregnancy. Between the years 1991 and 1997, when the number of sexually active high school students fell 11 percent, teen pregnancy rates experienced an unprecedented decline of 16 percent. According to a study conducted by the Consortium of State Physicians Resource Councils, this decline "is a result of the increase in the number of teens choosing abstinence."[2] It follows that in areas where abstinence programs are emphasized, the declines are even greater. The most remarkable case to date is an abstinence program instituted by Cathi Woods in Rhea County High School in Tennessee. Her program, which shows how premarital sex causes heartbreak among teens, has convinced many teens to remain virgins and others to stop engaging in sex. The result has been a striking improvement in teen pregnancy rates. According to Gary Thomas, a writer for *Christianity Today,*

> In just one year [after Woods's abstinence program was instituted] Rhea County dropped from being number one in teen pregnancies per capita in the state to tenth; during the second year, they dropped from tenth to forty-sixth and then, one year later, to sixty-fourth. Nothing else was done differently either in the school or community, except for Woods's [abstinence] program.[3]

The success of abstinence programs in preventing teen pregnancy recently drew attention from the federal government. In 1998, Congress signed a law allocating additional federal funds to sex-education programs that teach students abstinence and only abstinence. Unfortunately, some prominent sex educators, such as the Sexuality Information and

Education Council of the United States, dispute this law on the grounds that sex-education programs should promote contraception as well as teach abstinence. They call their approach "comprehensive sex education."

"Comprehensive" Sex Education Harms Teenagers

Comprehensive sex education sounds impressive at first. After all, why not try to cover all bases by teaching kids about abstinence *and* contraception? However, a closer examination of this ideology reveals that it is harmful to teens. First, providing teens with information about contraceptives—or worse, providing contraceptives themselves—sends a confusing dual message. Unlike abstinence programs, which communicate clearly that premarital sex is harmful and unethical, the message of comprehensive sex education programs contradicts itself. At the same time that these programs encourage abstinence, they are explicitly showing teens how *not* to be abstinent. Imagine if society sent similar messages to teens about other types of destructive behavior. Lakita Garth, a female performer and businesswoman who has remained a virgin into her twenties, explains how these messages would sound:

- Drugs are illegal, but since we know you're going to do it anyway, we're going to instruct you on how many cc's you can safely inject yourself with without overdosing. . . .

- Smoking is bad for you and it is illegal for someone to sell cigarettes to minors, but since we know you're going to do it anyway, we're going to provide filters for you at the school-based clinic. In addition, we'll even schedule appointments for you to purchase cigarettes without your parents' consent to protect your privacy.

- Carrying handguns is illegal for minors, but since we know you're going to do it anyway, we're going to provide a bulletproof vest distribution program. Moreover, we'll show you how to become expert marksmen so when you do your drive-bys you will be responsible enough not to shoot innocent babies and elderly people.[4]

The absurdity of these statements demonstrates the defective logic behind sex-education programs that attempt to promote both abstinence and contraception. However, this is exactly the type of logic that guides comprehensive sex education. Its message to teenagers is: "You shouldn't have sex, but if you choose to have it, use a condom." Endorsing contraception completely undermines any attempt to promote abstinence because it signals to teens that adults do not trust them to make the right decisions about sex.

No Such Thing as "Safe" Sex

Comprehensive sex education also harms teens by giving them false information about the effectiveness of contraception. These programs suggest that teenagers can have sex "safely" by using contraception and protection against sexually transmitted diseases. "Safe sex," however, is a widely publicized myth. The truth is that sex outside of marriage is always dangerous because it poses the threat of unwanted pregnancy and diseases that can cause infertility, birth defects, genital cancer, or even death. Many of these diseases, such as AIDS, the human papilloma virus (HPV), and herpes, have no cure.

To advocate condoms as a solution to these risks is irresponsible. First, condoms are completely ineffective unless they are used correctly every time—which most people cannot do. One study showed that *only 50 percent* of couples who knew one partner was infected with HIV, the virus that causes AIDS, managed perfect condom use within a two-year period. If half of these adult couples failed to use condoms correctly, one can only imagine the condom failure rate for teenagers. According to Joe S. McIlhaney Jr.,

Some studies have found that as few as 5 percent of sexually active teens consistently use condoms, and even the most optimistic have found that only 40 percent do. . . . No more than 50 percent of adolescents typically report that they use condoms correctly. A CDC study found that only half of sexually active high-school students used a condom the last time they had sex.[5]

Even those teens who do use condoms consistently and correctly are still at risk. As the National Coalition for Abstinence Education writes, "Condoms, even when used correctly, offer little or no protection against human papilloma virus (HPV) and only slightly better protection against chlamydia. . . . Further, about 15 percent of female adolescents using condoms get pregnant during the first year of use."[6]

Clearly, the message that contraception is the answer to teen pregnancy is putting more and more teens at grave risk. All of the evidence points to one conclusion: The only way for teenagers to be safe from disease and pregnancy is to abstain from sex. It is time for adults to communicate this in no uncertain terms.

1. Quoted in Tammy Busche, "Young People Commit to Sexual Purity as Part of 'True Love Waits' Campaign," *St. Charles County Post*, March 19, 1999, p. 1.

2. Renee Wixon, "Instead of Condoms, Let's Give Teens Help in Abstaining from Sex," *Star Tribune*, April 3, 1999, p. 17A.

3. Gary Thomas, "Where True Love Waits," *Christianity Today*, March 1, 1999, p. 40.

4. Lakita Garth, testimony given on July 16, 1998. *Hearings on the Social and Economic Costs of Teen Pregnancy Before the Empowerment Subcommittee of the Small Business Committee*. Washington, DC: U.S. Government Printing Office, 1998, p. 75.

5. Joe S. McIlhaney Jr., "Q: Are Abstinence-Only Sex-Education Programs Good for Children? Yes: 'Safe Sex' Education Has Failed. It's Time to Give Kids the Good News About Abstinence," *Insight*, September 29, 1997, p. 24.

6. National Coalition for Abstinence Education, "Frequently Asked Questions About the Title V Abstinence Education Program." On-line. Internet. Available at http://www.family.org/cforum/hptissues/A0001033.html.

"The increased use of condoms and other effective contraceptive practices 'account[s] for 80 percent of the decrease in teen pregnancy.'"

Promoting the Use of Birth Control Reduces Teen Pregnancy

Although the problem of teen pregnancy is far from being resolved, recent statistics show that society is making significant headway in curbing the problem. A comprehensive study published in 1998 by the National Center for Health Statistics reported that between the years 1991 to 1997, the teen birth rate has fallen 16 percent, the pregnancy rate among African American teens has dropped 20 percent, and the abortion rate is steadily declining.

The explanation for these improvements is simple: Today's teenagers are more likely than teens of the past to be using contraception. Many sexually active teens are demonstrating responsible behavior by using condoms, which protect against sexually transmitted diseases as well as pregnancy. According to Dr. Robert Blum, director of adolescent health at the University of Minnesota, society is experiencing "more than a fourfold increase in the use of condoms"[1] among teenagers since the mid-1980s, when only 11 percent of teenagers used condoms. Research conducted by the Alan Guttmacher Institute reports that the increased use of condoms and other effective contraceptive practices "account[s] for 80 percent of the decrease in teen pregnancy."[2]

"Abstinence-Only" Education

However, despite the fact that contraception has dramatically cut teen pregnancies, the government has made it virtually impossible for public schools to provide students with adequate information about contraception. As of 1998, federal funds for sex-education programs are given only to states who pledge to teach teenagers abstinence and who refuse to acknowledge birth control as a reliable means of preventing pregnancy. The new law defines "abstinence-only" education as that which

(A) has as its exclusive purpose, teaching the social, psychological, and health gains to be realized by abstaining from sexual activity;

(B) teaches abstinence from sexual activity outside marriage as the expected standard for all school age children;

(C) teaches that abstinence from sexual activity is the only certain way to avoid out-of-wedlock pregnancy, sexually transmitted diseases, and other associated health problems;

(D) teaches that a mutually faithful monogamous relationship in context of marriage is the expected standard of human sexual activity;

(E) teaches that sexual activity outside of the context of marriage is likely to have harmful psychological and physical effects;

(F) teaches that bearing children out-of-wedlock is likely to have harmful consequences for the child, the child's parents, and society;

(G) teaches young people how to reject sexual advances and how alcohol and drug use increases vulnerability to sexual advances;

(H) teaches the importance of attaining self-sufficiency before engaging in sexual activity.[3]

A Moralistic Agenda

With its self-righteous assertion that "a mutually faithful monogamous relationship in context of marriage is the expected standard of human sexual activity," this law holds teenagers to a standard—no sex outside of marriage—that only a handful of American adults follow. As Debra W. Haffner, president and chief executive officer of the Sexuality Information and Education Council of the United States, attests, "The vast majority of Americans begin having sexual relationships before marriage. According to the largest national scientific study of sexual behavior of adults, published in 1994, fewer than 7 percent of men and 20 percent of women age 18 to 59 were virgins when they married."[4]

Furthermore, the abstinence-only law suggests that it is wrong and harmful for the 74 million Americans who are single, gay, divorced, or widowed to have sex. This type of moralistic attitude betrays the true agenda of the abstinence-only movement: to restore the puritanical view that all sex outside of marriage is evil.

Teaching Abstinence Does Not Work

However, the abstinence-only movement has failed even in this respect. Researchers agree that abstinence-only programs do not change teens' attitudes toward sex. A 1997 study from the University of Nebraska-Lincoln, which analyzed more than two dozen abstinence-only programs, found that the majority had no effect on the timing or amount of teen sexual activity. Moreover, a study of the Education Now, Babies Later, a program that involves 187,000 teens in California, discovered that the program "had no impact on the age at which teenagers began to have sex."[5]

While abstinence-only programs do not prevent teens from having sex, they actually worsen the problem of teen pregnancy.

Most of these programs promote the false notion that contraceptives are not effective barriers against pregnancy, thus making it more likely that sexually active teens will not use any form of protection. Other programs refuse even to acknowledge that birth control exists—thus providing teens with a sure route to unwanted pregnancy.

A Comprehensive Approach

If promoters of abstinence-only sex education were truly interested in helping teenagers, they would admit that a comprehensive approach to sex education—what is sometimes referred to as "abstinence-plus"—is what works best to help teenagers stay healthy and complete school without becoming parents. Doug Kirby, a research scientist and a national expert on sex education issues, states that abstinence-plus means "you give real weight to abstinence, you give it serious attention, you say that abstinence is the only method that is 100 percent effective against pregnancy and sexually transmitted diseases. But then you also talk about condoms and contraception in a balanced and accurate manner."[6]

The most common objection to giving teenagers information about contraception is that it will encourage teens to become sexually active. This is untrue. As condom use among teens has risen, the percentage of teens who are sexually active has dropped. Kirby argues that "we have solid evidence that [contraception programs] do not [encourage teen sex]."[7] Furthermore, it should be obvious that teens who choose to abstain from sex will not suddenly change their minds merely because they are told about condoms.

In the same way, teens who want to have sex will hardly be deterred by programs that preach abstinence as the only option. What such programs *will* accomplish, however, is to endanger the lives and futures of sexually active teens. Abstinence-only supporters would stand back and watch while sexually active teens endure unwanted pregnancies or contract lethal diseases such as AIDS. The implicit message these programs send to sexually active teens is that they "deserve" any consequences

that result from having premarital sex. This is not pregnancy prevention; this is punishment.

Certainly sex is not an inevitable choice for many—or even the majority of—teens. However, it is naïve to think that every single teenager in America will abstain from sex. And as long as some teenagers are sexually active, society has a moral obligation to help them make their way safely through the difficult time of adolescence.

1. Quoted in Pat Wingert, "The Battle Over Falling Birth Rates," *Newsweek*, May 11, 1998, p. 40.

2. Quoted in Steve Trombley, "Sex Education Helps Cut Teen Pregnancies," *Chicago Sun-Times*, May 7, 1999, p. 52.

3. *United States Code Annotated Title 42. The Public Health and Welfare.* On-line. Internet. Available at http://www.tdh.texas.gov/abstain/federal.htm

4. Debra W. Haffner, "Are Abstinence-Only Sex-Education Programs Good for Teenagers? No: Abstinence-Only Education Isn't Enough. Teens Need a Wide Range of Information," *Insight*, September 29, 1997, p. 27.

5. Sharon Lerner, "Just Say No to Sex; Just Say Yes to Big Bucks," *Salon Magazine*, September 23, 1999. On-line. Internet. Available at http://www.salonmagazine.com/health/feature/1999/09/23/abstinence/index.html.

6. Quoted in E.J. Dionne, "An Argument for Abstinence-Plus," *Denver Post*, July 16, 1999, p. B9.

7. Quoted in Dionne, "An Argument for Abstinence-Plus," p. B9.

"Teens need to know that a baby is the last thing they want. They need to see that life after a baby is hard—darn hard."

Restoring Social Stigma Will Help Prevent Teen Pregnancy

Before the sexual revolution of the 1960s, society held a clear line on teen pregnancy. Becoming pregnant as a teenager, or getting someone else pregnant, was something to be ashamed about. Teenage girls tried hard not to become pregnant—many refused to have sex for this reason—and if they did, their options were limited. Because abortion was illegal and illegitimacy was socially unacceptable, a pregnant teen in the 1950s could either marry the father of her child or give up her baby for adoption. If she chose the latter, she was likely to have her baby in secret at an out-of-town relative's house to protect her family's and her own reputation. For everyone involved, teenage pregnancy was a serious embarrassment. As Mary A. Mitchell, columnist for the *Chicago Sun-Times*, writes,

> Pregnant teens were sent to an alternative school. If they were really lucky, they had a father who went looking for the dad-to-be and came back with his good

intentions. We all understood that teen pregnancy was the worst thing that could happen, and even the fastest girls would know to go to the neighborhood clinic for a supply of contraceptives.[1]

Simply put, the societal shame associated with teen pregnancy was so severe that it prevented many teens from becoming pregnant. Teens saw that pregnancy had immediate and unpleasant consequences, and so they were strongly motivated to avoid it. This is why fewer than 10 percent of teen births in 1950 were to unmarried teens.

Today, teen pregnancy carries little or no stigma. Society generally treats teen parents with solicitous concern, as if these teens were victims of circumstances beyond their control. In some cases, teen mothers are eligible for free parenting classes, daycare provided by their high schools, and even financial support from the government.

The fact that society is more tolerant of teen parenthood clearly benefits individual teen parents. However, this tolerant attitude has a negative impact on the issue of teen pregnancy as a whole. By eliminating the social stigma associated with teen pregnancy, society has ensured that more and more teens will become pregnant. The numbers are proof of this. Today, births to unmarried teens are over 75 percent of all teen births. One estimate attests that four out of ten American women become pregnant before the age of twenty. Teen pregnancy is no longer an aberration or an embarrassment; it is practically the norm.

Teen Pregnancy and the Sexual Revolution

How did society's values change so dramatically within such a short span of time? The sexual revolution is mostly to blame. Started by hippie youths in the 1960s, the sexual revolution popularized the notion that sex outside of marriage was acceptable. As a result, premarital sex and cohabitation among unmarried partners has become extremely common, while the traditional family has suffered. Today, marriage is considered to be almost superfluous to an intimate relationship, and is certainly not viewed as a prerequisite for parenthood.

Because so many people are having children outside of marriage, unwed pregnancy, even among teens, is no longer seen as wrong. Americans view teen pregnancy at worst as a bad choice—a bad choice so prevalent that it rarely inspires shock or disgust.

The result of these shifting norms is that many teens do not see any reason to prevent pregnancy. As sociologist Kristin Luker contends, "Although some teenagers try to prevent pregnancy and fail, others get pregnant because they believe pregnancy is not such a bad thing. Young unmarried women, like young married ones, may become pregnant because they want to."[2]

An Aura of Importance

In fact, with no social taboo against it, pregnancy looks like an appealing choice for many teens. Many teens want to become pregnant—or do not try to avoid it—because they see unwed pregnancy as something that will earn them attention and admiration from their peers. According to the National Campaign to Prevent Teen Pregnancy, when asked why teenagers become pregnant, many teens stated that "teenage mothers came to school 'bragging' about their babies and acted as if having a child gave them an elevated status."[3] One teen explains why teen moms have an aura of importance: "It makes it seem like they got money. Like they know what they're doing. They got more experience than any other girl. They come around there with their children in nice clothes and all the time making it seem like they got money, that they can get anything they want."[4]

Part of the reason motherhood seems so attractive to teens is because child care centers in public schools allow teen mothers to attend school like any other student. Instead of being ostracized from society, as they were in the 1950s, teen mothers now parade their babies around high school with pride. This causes other girls to see teen pregnancy as a normal and even glamorous lifestyle.

Restoring Social Stigma to Teen Pregnancy

Society must stop portraying teen pregnancy as normal. This means ending all programs intended to make life easier for teen mothers. Although this may seem cruel, it is far worse to let impressionable young girls think that pregnancy will give them positive attention. As Mitchell writes, "Proud teens pushing beautiful babies through the hallways . . . isn't . . . an image that most teen girls need to see. Teens need to know that a baby is the last thing they want. They need to see that life after a baby is hard—darn hard."[5]

Obviously, most teens are too immature and inexperienced to see for themselves why pregnancy is a bad choice. It is up to society, then, to discourage teens from making that choice. The only way to convince teens not to become pregnant is for society as a whole to condemn teen pregnancy as irresponsible and immoral behavior. Judge Judy, the television judge famous for telling it like it is, says it best: "Teen pregnancy is stupid. Never mind immoral, wasteful or unhealthy. . . . We should tell [teenagers] that a girl who gets pregnant is dumb. . . . A fool."[6] As long as teenagers think otherwise, any effort to prevent teen pregnancy, no matter how well conceived, will be futile.

1. Mary A. Mitchell, "Pregnant? No Problem," *Chicago Sun-Times*, June 11, 1998, p. 35.

2. Kristin Luker, *Dubious Conceptions: The Politics of Teen Pregnancy*. Cambridge, MA: Harvard University Press, 1996, p. 151.

3. National Campaign to Prevent Teen Pregnancy, *What About the Teens? Research on What Teens Say About Teen Pregnancy. A Focus Group Report*. April 1999, p. 10.

4. Quoted in National Campaign to Prevent Teen Pregnancy, *What About Teens?*, p. 11.

5. Mitchell, "Pregnant? No Problem," p. 35.

6. Quoted in Trisha Flynn, "Attitude Plus Access Equals Success," *Denver Post*, June 6, 1999, p. G-03.

STUDY QUESTIONS

Chapter 1

1. Viewpoint 2, contending that the problem of teen pregnancy is decreasing, cites statistics about the decline in teen pregnancy and motherhood. How does Viewpoint 1 refute these statistics? Whose interpretation is more persuasive, and why?

2. According to Viewpoint 1, why should society be extremely concerned about teen pregnancy? Are these concerns valid, in your opinion, or are they the result of media hype, as argued by Viewpoint 2? Support your answer.

3. Viewpoint 3 provides quotations from teens who regret becoming mothers at a young age, while Viewpoint 4 provides quotations from teens who are happy to be parents. Which quotes are more convincing, in your opinion? Can parenthood be a positive choice for teens under some circumstances? Why or why not?

4. Based on what you have read in this chapter, is teen pregnancy a serious problem for teens and society as a whole? What specific arguments offered by the viewpoints influence your answer?

Chapter 2

1. According to the viewpoints in this chapter, what characteristics—economic, social, and emotional—make teens more likely to become pregnant?

2. Based on what you have read in this chapter, what role do adults play in the problem of teen pregnancy?

3. For each of the causes of teen pregnancy examined in this chapter, explain what steps the government, communities, and individuals could take to combat these causes.

4. How would you prioritize the causes of teen pregnancy discussed in this chapter in terms of importance? Give specific reasons for your answer.

Chapter 3

1. What contrasting assumptions do Viewpoints 1 and 2 make about teenagers and sex? Which of these assumptions do you agree with and why?

2. Compare the use of statistics in Viewpoint 1 and Viewpoint 2. Which viewpoint uses statistics more effectively? Explain your answer.

3. According to Viewpoint 3, how would stigmatizing teenage pregnancy prevent teens from becoming pregnant? What negative consequences might such a stigma have?

APPENDIX A

Facts About Teen Pregnancy

Facts About Teen Sex
—Eight in ten girls and seven in ten boys are virgins at age fifteen.
—Half of seventeen-year-olds have had sexual intercourse.
—The younger a teenage girl begins having intercourse, the more likely she is to have had unwanted sex.
—One in four sexually active teens acquire a sexually transmitted disease.
—A sexually active teenager who does not use contraception has a 90 percent chance of becoming pregnant within a year.

Teen Pregnancy Statistics
—The teen birth rate declined 12 percent during the years 1991 to 1996.
—The United States has the highest rates of teen pregnancy and births in the Western industrialized world.
—Approximately 1 million U.S. teenagers become pregnant each year.
—Thirteen percent of all U.S. births are to teenagers.
—More than four out of ten American women become pregnant at least once before they reach the age of twenty. Eight in ten of these pregnancies are unintended.
—Eighty percent of teen pregnancies are to unmarried teens.
—Among sexually active teens, approximately 8 percent of fourteen-year-olds, 18 percent of fifteen- to seventeen-year-olds, and 22 percent of eighteen- to nineteen-year-olds become pregnant each year.
—Nearly four in ten teen pregnancies end in abortion.
—Teen childbearing costs taxpayers approximately $7 billion a year.

Facts About Teen Mothers and Their Children
—Teen mothers are less likely to earn a high school diploma.
—Teen mothers have an increased risk of experiencing poverty.
—Twenty-five percent of teen mothers have a second baby within two years of the first baby's birth.
—The children of teen mothers are more likely to have problems in school and experience abuse and neglect.
—The daughters of teen mothers are 22 percent more likely to become teen mothers themselves.
—The sons of teen mothers are 13 percent more likely to end up in prison.

APPENDIX B

Related Documents

Document 1: Preventing Teen Pregnancy: Messages for Teens and Parents

The following document, written by the National Campaign to Prevent Teen Pregnancy, provides teens and adults with specific tactics for preventing teen pregnancy. Founded in 1996 and formally launched in May 1997, the National Campaign to Prevent Teen Pregnancy is a nonprofit organization that seeks to reduce the teen pregnancy rate by one-third between 1996 and 2005.

Messages for Teens

1. *Just because you think "everyone else is doing it," doesn't mean they are. Some are, some aren't—and some are lying.* Of all teens under 20, about half have had sex and half have not. Most younger teens have not had sex—only about a quarter of 15-year-olds are sexually experienced. And among teens who have had sex, most report that they wish they had waited longer to begin having sex. It's okay to delay.

2. *There are only two ways to avoid pregnancy: either don't have sex at all, or use birth control very carefully, every single time. Choose one strategy or the other.* Right now, too many teens are doing neither one, and the result is that the U.S. has the highest rate of teen pregnancy in the industrialized world. 30% of sexually active teen girls (age 15–19) did not use contraception/birth control the last time they had sex. *A sexually active teen who does not use contraception has a 90% chance of pregnancy within one year.*

3. *You can always say "no"—even if you've said yes before.* Just because you have had sex with someone, doesn't mean you have to have sex in every relationship after that. You don't even have to continue having sex with your current partner if you don't want to. You always have the power to say no, regardless of your sexual history or your "reputation."

4. *Being prepared for sex doesn't make you pushy or easy—it makes you smart.* Think about how to handle a sexual situation *before* you're in the middle of one. Sex happens—plan what you will do in the moment. Will you insist on waiting for sex? Use contraception? Which method? How will you say no without hurting someone's feelings?

5. *It only takes once.* One of the most common myths among teens is that pregnancy can't happen the "first time." *In fact, 20 percent of first teen pregnancies happen in the* first month *of sexual activity*, and 50 percent of first pregnancies happen in the first six months of sexual activity.

6. *If you're drunk or high, you can't make good decisions about sex.* Alcohol and/or drug use makes teens more likely to have unplanned or even unwanted sex. And having sex while drunk or high means teens are much

less likely to use protection. This leads to higher risks of HIV, STDs, and pregnancy. *A survey of high school students found that 30% of boys and 18% of girls said it's OK for a boy to force sex if a girl is stoned or drunk.* If you see your friends losing control, help them avoid risky situations.

7. *(Teen girls) Sex won't make him yours, and a baby won't make him stay.* One of the worst reasons to have sex is because you think your boyfriend will dump you if you don't. Sex and pregnancy don't guarantee a lasting, loving relationship—in fact, 80% of teen fathers don't marry the teen mothers of their children. If sex is the price of a relationship, find someone else.

8. *(For boys) Boys can say no too. You don't have to have sex to prove anything to your friends or girlfriends.* Many teen boys feel pressure to have sex from their peers as well as their girlfriends, and some feel pressure to get their girlfriends pregnant. Many teen boys who had early sex say that, looking back, they wish they'd waited. *Having sex does not make you a man: waiting until you're ready and acting responsibly does.*

9. *(For older teens) Younger teens are listening to you more than to anyone else.* Talk with your little sister or brother, a neighbor, someone at school—seek them out and let them know they can ask you anything. Kids who have positive, close relationships with their siblings are less likely to take risks with sex.

Messages for Parents and Teen-Involved Adults

1. *Teens want to know what adults think. Even if they don't act like it.* Adults are powerful figures in the lives of young people and hold the key to preventing teen pregnancy. An MTV poll found teens ranked their parents as their #1 heroes.

2. *Forget about "The Talk." It is an eighteen-year conversation about love, relationships, values, and sex. Start early and let your kids know that you are an "askable parent."* Teens tell us their parents tend to give them information too late and in too vague a way. They can get clinical information from school or books (and they already know more than you think), but what they really seek is parents who are comfortable talking with them about relationships, how to handle peer pressure to have sex, how to say "no" without hurting feelings, and other such issues.

3. *Don't let your daughter get involved with a much older guy.* Teen girls who date much older guys are less likely to use birth control/contraception, and are more likely to report later that they didn't really want to have sex in the first place. Among mothers aged 15–17, about one in four has a partner who is at least *5 years older.* Older boys and men can lead younger girls into very risky situations and relationships.

4. *Sometimes, all it takes for teens not to have sex is not to have the opportunity.* Many teens say that if they have something to do after school that's fun and interesting, they are less likely to experiment with sex, drinking, and other risky activities. Some kids are having sex because there's nothing better to do. If parents can't be home with kids after school, they need to make sure their

kids are busy doing something constructive and engaging.

5. *Parents need to make girls feel valued and important.* You can't give a girl self-esteem, but you can give her the opportunity to develop it—encourage her involvement in sports, volunteering, drama classes, or other activities that make her feel talented and confident. *Girls involved in sports are half as likely to get pregnant as non-athletes, regardless of how much sex education they have.* They are more likely to delay sex until they are older, and to use protection when they do so. Another study shows that *girls who are active volunteers thoughout their high school years have half the teen pregnancy rates* of the average for their peers. If you give a girl something positive to say "yes" to, she'll be much more likely to say "no, not yet" to sex and pregnancy.

6. *Talk to sons as well as daughters. The nearly one million teen girls who got pregnant last year [1998] didn't do it alone.* Boys need to know that teen pregnancy happens to them too. We need to talk to boys—not just girls—about consequences, responsibility, sex, love, and values. Surveys show that boys want to do the right thing. *Help boys understand that they must do whatever it takes to be sure they don't get someone pregnant.*

http://www.teenpregnancy.org/teen/messages.html. Reprinted by permission of The National Campaign to Prevent Teen Pregnancy.

Document 2: National Vital Statistics Report: Declines in Teenage Birth Rates, 1991–97

Recent data from the National Center for Health Statistics (NCHS) reveals that teenage birth rates have declined during the 1990s. The subsequent document is an excerpt from the 1998 NCHS report.

The birth rate for U.S. teenagers in 1997 was 52.9 live births per 1,000 women aged 15–19 years, 3 percent lower than in 1996, and 15 percent lower than in 1991 (figure 1). The rate of 62.1 reported for 1991 was the highest level recorded in 20 years (64.5 in 1971). While the teenage birth rate has fallen steadily in the 1990's, the rate in 1997 remains higher than the rates in the mid-1980's, when they were at their lowest point ever (50 to 51 per 1,000).

The teenage birth rate declined fairly steadily from the late 1950's to the mid-1980's. Rates in the late 1950's were the highest ever recorded with the peak rate reported in 1957, at 96.3 births per 1,000. After reaching a low point in the mid-1980's, the teenage birth rate climbed steeply, with an overall increase of 24 percent between 1986 (50.2 per 1,000) and 1991 (62.1). The current downward trend represents a reversal of that increase.

While several measures are appropriate for examining patterns of teenage childbearing, the most useful measure is the birth rate, defined as the number of live births per 1,000 teenagers. This measure enables us to compare levels and trends in teenage childbearing among different population groups and over time for the same group, because all rates are computed on the basis of 1,000 women. For example, the birth rate for teenagers 15–17 years in 1997 was 32.6 births per 1,000 women aged 15–17 years. That rate was 38.7 in 1991. The *rate* for this age group has dropped 16 percent from 1991 to 1997 (table A). The number of births indicates how many teenagers gave birth in a given year. It is affected by the birth rate for a given age group (that is, the proportion of teenagers giving birth) and the number of females of that age. Looking again at teenagers 15–17 years, the number of births in 1997 was 183,324, compared with 188,226 in 1991, a modest reduction of about 3 percent. The number of births did not fall as much as the birth rate because the number of female

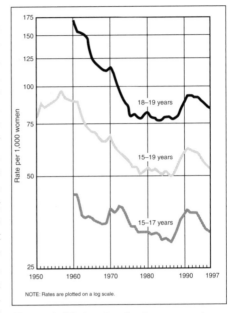

Figure 1. Birth rates for teenagers by age: United States, 1950–97

teenagers in the population increased 16 percent from 1991 to 1997.

Unmarried Births Are a Larger Proportion of All Teenage Births

Teenagers have never married in large numbers; however, the proportion who are married now is at a record low. In 1970 about 10 percent of female teenagers were married; a quarter century later, this proportion fell to less than 5 percent. Since 1970 the birth rate for married teenagers declined more than 20 percent (from 443.7 per 1,000 married women aged 15–19 years in 1970 to

Table A. Births and birth rates for teenagers by age: United States, 1991–97

[Birth rates per 1,000 women in specified age group]

Year	Number of births			Birth Rate		
	10–14 years	15–17 years	18–19 years	10–14 years	15–17 years	18–19 years
1997	10,852	183,324	305,886	1.2	32.6	84.4
1996	11,148	185,721	305,856	1.2	33.8	86.0
1995	12,242	192,508	307,365	1.3	36.0	89.1
1994	12,801	191,169	310,319	1.4	37.6	91.5
1993	12,554	190,535	310,558	1.4	37.8	92.1
1992	12,220	187,549	317,866	1.4	37.8	94.5
1991	12,015	188,226	331,351	1.4	38.7	94.4
Percent change, 1991	-9.7	-2.6	-7.7	-14.3	-158.8	-10.6

[1]Data for 1997 are preliminary.

344.3 in 1996). At the same time the birth rate for unmarried teenagers doubled, with most of the increase coming in the 1980's. The rate rose from 22.4 per 1,000 in 1970 to 46.4 in 1994, and has since declined 8 percent (42.9 in 1996). Because of these changes in marriage patterns among teenagers and birth rates for unmarried and married teenagers, the proportion of teenage births occurring to unmarried women has risen steeply (figure 2). For example, among teenage mothers 15–17 years, the proportion unmarried more than doubled, from 43 percent in 1970 to 87 percent in 1997. Similarly, among teenage mothers 18–19 years, the proportion unmarried more than tripled from 22 percent in 1970 to 72 percent in 1997.

These major changes in marriage and marital and nonmarital birth rates are not unique to teenagers. In fact, relatively fewer women in all age groups are married nowadays, and birth rates have increased sharply for unmarried women in all age groups. As a consequence, while most births to teenagers are nonmarital, teenagers do not account for the majority of all births to unmarried women. As recently as 1975, more than half of all births to unmarried women were to teenagers; by 1997, the proportion under age 20 was only 31 percent.

Teenage Birth and Pregnancy Rates Fall

In order to examine trends in *pregnancies* among teenagers, data on live births must be combined with data on induced abortions and fetal losses. Because information on abortion and fetal loss is not as current as information on live births, this report focuses on trends and variations in live births and live birth rates. However, recent abortion data indicate that the current decline in teenage *birth* rates has been accompanied by declines in abortion rates as well; thus teenage *pregnancy* rates have fallen in the 1990's. According to the most recent complete estimates, the teenage pregnancy rate declined 12 percent from 1991 to 1995. The pregnancy rate for 1995 was 103 pregnancies per 1,000 women aged 15–19 years, nearly twice the birth rate in that year (56.8). In 1976 these rates were 101 (pregnancy) and 53 (live birth).

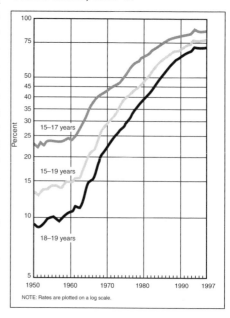

Figure 2. Percent of births to unmarried teenagers by age: United States, 1950–97

NOTE: Rates are plotted on a log scale.

Birth Rates Decline for Teenagers in All Age Groups

The live birth rate for the youngest teenagers, *10–14 years*, fell to 1.2 per 1,000 in 1997. This rate declined from 1.4 in 1990–94 to 1.3 in 1995 and 1.2 in 1996–97. Concurrent with the decline in the birth *rate*, the number of births to this age group has fallen as well, dropping from an average of 12,000–13,000 per year in 1991–95, to under 11,000 in 1997 (table A).

The birth rate for teenagers *15–17 years* fell 4 percent between 1996 and 1997 to 32.6 per 1,000. Overall, this rate fell 16 percent from 1991 (38.7) to 1997. Sixty percent of the decline occurred from 1995 to 1997. The long-term trend for this age group has not been as steady as for older teenagers (figure 1). The rate generally declined from the early 1970's to the mid-1980's, before climbing 27 percent from 1986 to 1991, and then declining to its current level. The number of births to teenagers 15–17 years totaled 183,324 in 1997. This number did not begin to decline steadily until after 1994. The decline in the number of births is smaller than the decline in the birth rate because, as noted earlier, the number of female teenagers in the population has increased by 16 percent, since 1991.

The birth rate for teenagers *18–19 years* declined 2 percent from 1996 to 1997 to 84.4 per 1,000. This rate fell 11 percent from 1991 to 1997. The birth rate for 18–19-year-olds declined rapidly from 1960 (166.7 per 1,000) to the late 1970's, where it stabilized at about 80 per 1,000, less than half the 1960 rate. Beginning in the late 1980's, this rate began to increase, rising 20 percent during 1987–92, and then falling again. The number of births to teenagers 18–19 years was 305,886 in 1997, about the same as in 1996 (305,856). This number declined from 1990 (338,499).

The number of births to teenagers, like the teenage birth rate, was substantially higher several decades ago than now. The peak number of births was reported in 1970, with 644,708 babies born to women aged 15–19 years. The 1970 total is nearly a third higher than in 1997.

Despite Declines, Black and Hispanic
Teenage Birth Rates Are Still High

Birth rates have dropped sharply for black teenagers (by 23 percent) from 115.5 per 1,000 aged 15–19 years in 1991 to 89.5 in 1997. The rate for Hispanic teenagers has declined since 1994, by 8 percent. Birth rates for black and Hispanic teenagers continue to be substantially higher than for other racial groups (figure 3). All race and Hispanic origin groups have experienced declines in teenage birth rates in the 1990's. Declines for non-Hispanic white and American Indian teenagers were 16 percent each to 36.4 and 71.8 per 1,000, respectively. The rate for Asian or Pacific Islander teenagers, already the lowest of all, declined 10 percent since 1991—to 24.8 per 1,000.

In general, rates fell more for younger than for older teenagers. The largest reduction of all was the rate for black teenagers 15–17 years, dropping 26 percent from 84.1 to 62.3. Rates by age for Hispanic and Asian or

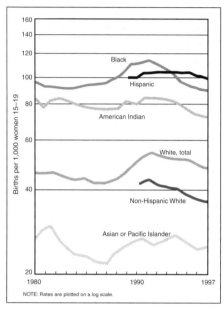

NOTE: Rates are plotted on a log scale.

Figure 3. Birth rate for teenagers 15–19 by race and Hispanic origin: United States, 1980–97

Pacific Islander teenagers declined more for older than for younger women. Beginning in 1994, Hispanic teenagers had higher birth rates than any other group (figure 3).

Fewer Teenagers Have Their First Baby

Birth rates for teenagers can also be calculated for teenagers who have not had a live birth and for teenagers with a previous live birth. The birth rate for teenagers who have not had a live birth describes the proportion of teenagers who give birth for the first time. More commonly, first birth rates are computed by relating first births to all women in a given age group, regardless of whether or not they have had any children. The rate for childless women enables us to measure precisely changes in first time childbearing among teenagers who have not yet had a child. It is thus a refinement of the first birth rate. For teenagers, the differences between the first birth rate and the birth rate for childless teenagers are relatively small and the trends are fairly similar, because most teenagers have not had any children. For example, the *first birth rate* for teenagers 15–19 years declined from 46.5 in 1991 to 42.5 in 1996, a reduction of 9 percent. The *birth rate for childless teenagers* declined from 49.6 in 1991 to 46.7 in 1996, a reduction of 6 percent.

Birth rates for teenagers who have not had a live birth increase sharply with age, as would be expected. The rate for childless teenagers 15 years was 17.1 per 1,000 in 1996, compared with a rate of 77.4 for childless teenagers 19 years. Unlike the overall teenage birth rate which has fallen steadily since 1991, the rate for childless teenagers did not begin to fall consistently until after 1994.

Even Fewer Teenagers Have a Second Child

In contrast to the modest declines in birth rates for teenagers who have not had a live birth, repeat childbearing, that is, the rate of second births to teenagers who have already had one child has fallen substantially since 1991. Repeat births are of particular concern; a teenager with two or more children is at greater risk for a host of difficulties. The rate of second order births to teenagers who have had one child dropped 21 percent to 174 per 1,000 aged 15–19 years in 1996, from 221 per 1,000 in 1991. To put it another way, 17 percent of teenagers who have had one child gave birth to a second child in 1996, compared with 22 percent in 1991. Rates fell for teenagers at each age 16 through 19 years, with the reductions much steeper for the youngest teenagers (figure 4). (The most recent year for which birth rates can be computed according to the number of previous births to the mother is 1996.)

Twenty-two percent of teenage births were second and higher order births in 1997, compared with 25 percent in 1991. Despite the reduction in repeat childbearing, over 100,000 teenagers gave birth to their second or higher order child in 1997.

The proportion of repeat births for young teenagers 15–17 years fell 20 percent from 1991 to 1997, from 15 to 12 percent; for young black teenagers, the proportion fell by 27 percent, from 22 percent to 16 percent. The proportion of second and higher order births for older teenagers 18–19 years declined 10 percent (from 31 to 28 percent); again, the proportion fell more for black teenagers, by 14 percent (from 42 to 36 percent).

Teenage Childbearing Has Serious Health Consequences

Teenage mothers and their babies are at greater risk of adverse health consequences compared with older mothers. Most teenage mothers are not ready for the emotional, psychological, and financial responsibilities and challenges of parenthood. The vast majority of teenage pregnancies are unintended. Teenagers who become pregnant are less likely to receive timely prenatal care and more likely to begin care in the third trimester or have no care at all (figure 5). They are also more likely to smoke during pregnancy. Moreover, a recent report showed that in contrast to declines in smoking for older women, smoking has increased among pregnant teenagers in the mid-1990's, concurrent with increases reported for all teenagers. As a consequence of these and other factors, infants born to teenagers are more likely to be born preterm, that is, at less than 37 completed weeks of gestation, and more likely to be low birthweight (less than 5 lb 8 oz), and thus are at greater risk of serious and long-term illness, developmental delays, and of dying in the first year of life. . . .

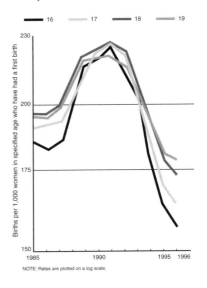

Figure 4. Rate of second births to teenagers who have had a first birth, 1985–96

NOTE: Rates are plotted on a log scale.

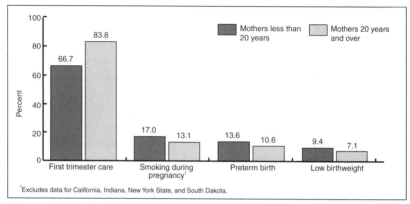

Figure 5. Selected characteristics for teenage mothers and mothers aged 20 years and over: United States, 1996

Declines in Sexual Activity and Increases in Condom Use Are Key Factors

The declines in birth and pregnancy rates for teenagers across the country since 1991 reflect changes in a number of demographic and behavioral factors. First, three separate surveys have shown that the proportion of teenagers who are sexually experienced has stabilized and declined in the 1990's, reversing the steady increases over the past two decades. According to results from the 1995 National Survey of Family Growth (NSF), conducted by the National Center for Health Statistics, and the National Survey of Adolescent Males (NSAM), the proportion of teenagers who are sexually experienced has fallen in the 1990's. More recently, results from the Youth Risk Behavior Surveillance Survey, conducted by the Centers for Disease Control and Prevention, show that among teenagers attending school, sexual activity has declined in the 1990's through 1997. Moreover, teenagers are more likely to use contraceptives at first intercourse, especially condoms. In addition, some teenagers, especially black teenagers, are using injectable and implant contraceptives. These changes in contraceptive use in particular are probably important factors in the decline in rates for second births to women who already have one child.

Teenage pregnancy has been the subject of a great deal of public interest and concern, especially since the late 1980's when rates increased rapidly. As a result, a variety of national, State, and local initiatives and strategies have been developed to reduce teenage pregnancy. Only a few programs have been rigorously evaluated and no single approach has been identified. However, findings from the National Longitudinal Study on Adolescent Health (Add Health), a large-scale, congressionally mandated survey of students in grade 7 through 12, have suggested that enhancing the connections of teenagers to their family and home, their school, and their community is essential for protecting teenagers from a vast array of risky behaviors, including sexual activity.

Stephanie J. Ventura, T. J. Mathews, and Sally C. Curtin, "Declines in Teenage Birth Rates, 1991–97: National and State Patterns," *National Vital Statistics Report*, December 17, 1998. Available at http://www.cdc.gov/nchs.

Document 3: Explaining the Decline in Teen Pregnancy Rates

The following document is excerpted from testimony given before the House Committee on Ways and Means June 1999 hearing on nonmarital births. The testimony was presented by Cory L. Richards, vice president of the Alan Guttmacher Institute, which supports teens' access to comprehensive sex education. Richards argues that teen pregnancy rates declined throughout the 1990s both because more sexually active teens used contraception and because more teens abstained from sex.

After years of steady increases, U.S. teen pregnancy rates have dropped markedly this decade. Teen pregnancy rates peaked in 1990, and then fell 17% between 1990 and 1996. Likewise, teen birthrates have fallen off since 1990, and teen abortion rates fell by almost a third between 1986 and 1996. . . .

Why have teen pregnancy rates fallen? Answers to this question are crucial, as they can—and should—inform how we can sustain these positive trends among teenagers, as well as shed much-needed light on ways to address the phenomenon of unintended pregnancy that is shared by women of all ages.

Careful analyses of key government data indicate that approximately 80% of the declines that we have seen in teen pregnancy can be attributed to declines in pregnancy rates among sexually experienced teenagers. Indeed, the drop in pregnancy rates among sexually experienced teens has been very marked—16% between 1990 and 1996. . . .

Government data do not bear out a decrease in levels of sexual activity among sexually experienced teens. On the other hand, there is evidence that a slightly larger proportion of sexually active teens are using contraceptives, and—even more significantly—that teens who do use contraceptives are using more effective methods. Most notably, there has been a substantial shift among sexually active teens toward use of highly effective, long-acting contraceptive methods—the contraceptive injectable, Depo-Provera and the contraceptive implant, Norplant. These methods only hit the U.S. market in the early 1990s, but by 1995, one in ten sexually active teen women at risk of unintended pregnancy was using one of them. Because these long-acting methods are so effective and so easy to use, they are making a big dent in the teen pregnancy rate. . . .

Our analyses additionally confirm that there has been a decline—or at least a leveling off—in the proportion of teenagers who have ever had sexual intercourse. Indeed, the proportion of women aged 15–19 who report they have ever had sexual intercourse decreased about one percentage point between 1988 and 1995. About 20% of the declines in the overall U.S. teen pregnancy rate is attributable to this increased abstinence.

Many questions remain around why teen contraceptive use has improved, and why more teens are remaining abstinent, but the bottom line is that both phenomena are making a difference in combating teen pregnancy. As we have seen, about 20% of that difference is attributable to increased abstinence; about 80% is due to more successful pregnancy prevention efforts among teens who are sexually active. This strongly suggests that even as abstinence is being promoted to our nation's young people, access to contraceptives for those teens who are sexually active—half of all U.S. teens—is also vitally important to reducing teen pregnancies, fully eight in ten of which are unintended.

In fact, access to highly effective contraceptives can—and clearly does—make a difference in reducing unintended pregnancy and, as a result, nonmarital births among all women.

Cory L. Richards, testimony before the Subcommittee on Human Resources of the House Committee on Ways and Means, Hearing on Nonmarital Births, June 29, 1999.

Document 4: Advice from the "Chastity Lady"

In the document that follows, Molly Kelly, who counsels American and international teens on the importance of postponing sex until marriage, explains to the Senate Appropriations Committee why she believes that sex education must promote abstinence.

Good afternoon. I am honored and excited to have this opportunity to address this Senate Appropriations Committee on the importance of funding abstinence centered education.

Let me begin by giving you a thumbnail sketch of who I am, what I do, and why I do it. I am Molly Kelly, the mother of 8, the grandmother of 9, the widow of the late Dr. Jim Kelly, a Philadelphia physician who believed in young people, and wanted to help them be healthy and happy, but his life was cut short by a tragic sledding accident. I am a lover of young people and have the privilege of speaking to over 100,000 each year throughout the United States, Canada, and indeed the world. This time last year [1996] I was in Australia where I had the privilege of speaking in 17 cities, to over 13,000 teens. And the reason I do all of this is because I believe in them and in their ability to live chaste lives . . . to practice abstinence . . . to save sex for marriage, and if they have already had sex, I invite them to start saving again! I am known as the chastity lady!

I use the word chastity because it gives young people boundaries, limits, and it has to do with the whole person, not just the sexual act. I definitely believe in teaching young people abstinence, but I think we need to elaborate on that word so that it will include such things as what they are willing to put in their minds, via the movies, television, CD's, and radio, and also what they allow to come out of their mouths. I am a firm believer in the "garbage in, garbage out" theory.

We tell young people to say no to drugs because drugs are harmful, whether they are married or single. I do not like to put sex in the negative category. Using drugs to get high is wrong, sex is not wrong. But using people . . . having sex with someone because it feels good and involves no commitment, is wrong and harmful.

My message to teens is a positive one. I tell them that they are so good, they are worth waiting for . . . and that sex is so good, it's worth waiting for. And I assure them that it's not the weekend I'm talking about as far as waiting, but marriage!

I find that it is too often the adults who cave in on the kids because of a preconceived built-in failure notion of them . . . the "What else can we do because they're going to do it anyway" mentality, "so let's save some of them by teaching them to use 'protection' when they have sex."

Much of the material used in public school health classes, that I have seen, or been apprised of, have emphasized the "safe sex" message, which promotes pills and condoms as protective measures . . . showing them pictures of the apparatus, and graphic descriptions of how they work, while the abstinence message is given a half-hearted nod, with no pictures, no suggestions on how to say no, and no talk of positive peer pressure. Instead, it tells them, "While abstinence is the only 100 percent protection, we know that some of you are going to engage in sex anyway, so here is the second best answer," and the teens are then encouraged to use the tools to have sex, when everyone knows that it is sex that causes pregnancy, sexually transmitted disease, and emotional damage, not the failure to use pills, condoms and devices!

And since when are our young people worth the second best answer! And, can we put the word *best* on things that have a known failure rate, and in the case of AIDS, the failure could mean death! Doesn't that sound like sexual roulette to you!

"Safe sex" does not ask young people to change their sexual behavior and therefore the statistics on teen pregnancy (1.2 million each year); teens with STDs (3 million each year); teen abortions (400,000 each year); and teens with the deadly AIDS virus (now the No. 1 killer of young adults in the United States); not to mention the devastating emotional damage to teens from engaging in premarital sex; will not decrease, but rather increase because too many adults want to treat the problem rather than solve it. Promoting "safe sex" is giving them the tools to do the very thing that causes the problems we want them to avoid.

And, it is an insult to their integrity, an assault on their character, and it has become a self-fulfilled prophecy. If you tell a child he is ugly, he thinks he's ugly. If you tell a child she is dumb, she feels dumb. And, if we tell a generation of young people that they can't say no, or that they don't have to as long as they use "protection" that may or may not work, then the results are and will continue to be devastating.

Senators, here's how it translates to teens.

They hear a health teacher tell them:

"Don't take drugs, you can control yourself!"

"Don't drink, you can control yourself!"

"Don't smoke, you can control yourself!"

"But when it comes to sex, you can't control yourself! Guys, use a condom, and girls, use a drug!" The birth control pill is a drug . . . a prescription drug.

And if this sounds confusing . . . it is!

I'd like to insert here that I have offered my home to 5 pregnant girls over a course of 7 years, and I can tell you that the tears they shed were . . . fear, frustration, anger, loneliness, rejection, heartbreak, despair . . . and all the condoms and the birth control pills in the world can't protect them from those wounds.

I would like to share with you what some teens have said to me after my talk. One young man asked me if I had a video. He told me that his Mom had died and that I reminded him of her, and he wanted his little brother to hear what his mother would have said. A young black teen in Orlando, Florida, told me that he was surprised that I didn't "drop the bomb" at the end of my talk. When I asked him what he meant, he said, "You didn't offer us condoms at the end." He saw that as a mixed message, and a destructive one. One young girl came up to me and said, "Thanks, I'm going to rewrap my gift and start saving it again."

There is a group of African American teens in Philadelphia who call themselves C.O.U.R.T., Chaste, Outstanding, Urban, Righteous Teens, and they formed because 9 public schools in the inner city began to offer condoms in schools, and these kids felt insulted!

I am a one shot deal to some people, but I see myself as a cheer leader for abstinence. I have been the kickoff speaker for the "It's Great To Wait" Program in South Carolina, and the "Campaign For Our Kids" abstinence program in Indiana. I was a grant reviewer for the Title XX Program that funded such great abstience programs as "Sex Respect," "Teen Aid," and "Teen Choice," and I work closely with Kathleen Sullivan and her very successful "Project Reality" abstinence program. In fact, Kathleen just told me that they have 9,000 teens signed up for the program this fall.

We need programs like these that teach young people to respect their sexuality and the sexuality of everyone they meet. Teens need the tools to say no and these programs do that. I urge, implore and beg you to fund abstinence education so that every young person in every single school can learn that they are worth waiting for! . . .

We want our young people to grow up happy and healthy, regardless of their religion, ethnic backgrouned, age, sex, or place of residence. Abstinence/chastity is good for all young people!

Molly Kelly, testimony, *Hearings Before a Subcommittee of the Committee on Appropriations, United States Senate, One Hundred Fourth Congress, Second Session.* Washington, DC: U.S. Government Printing Office, 1997.

ORGANIZATIONS TO CONTACT

The editors have compiled the following list of organizations concerned with the issues debated in this book. The descriptions are derived from materials provided by the organizations. All have publications or information available for interested readers. The list was compiled on the date of publication of the present volume; the information provided here may change. Be aware that many organizations take several weeks or longer to respond to inquiries, so allow as much time as possible.

Advocates for Youth
1025 Vermont Ave. NW, Suite 200
Washington, DC 20005
202/347-5700
fax: 202/347-2263
e-mail: info@advocatesforyouth.org
website: http://www.advocatesforyouth.org/

Formerly the Center for Population Options, Advocates for Youth is the only national organization focusing solely on pregnancy and HIV prevention among young people. It provides information, education, and advocacy to youth-serving agencies and professionals, policy makers, and the media. Among the organization's numerous publications are the brochures *Advice from Teens on Buying Condoms* and *Spread the Word — Not the Virus* and the pamphlet *How to Prevent Date Rape: Teen Tips.*

Alan Guttmacher Institute
120 Wall St.
New York, NY 10005
212/248-1111
fax: 212/248-1951
e-mail: info@agi-usa.org

The institute works to protect and expand the reproductive choices of all women and men. It strives to ensure people's access to the information and services they need to exercise their rights and responsibilities concerning sexual activity, reproduction, and family planning. Among the institute's publications are the books *Teenage Pregnancy in Industrialized Countries* and *Today's Adolescents, Tomorrow's Parents: A Portrait of the Americas* and the report, "Sex and America's Teenagers."

Child Trends, Inc. (CT)
4301 Connecticut Ave. NW, Suite 100
Washington, DC 20008
202/362-5580
fax: 202/362-5533
website: http://www.childtrends.org

CT works to provide accurate statistical and research information regarding children and their families in the United States and to educate the American public on the ways existing social trends, such as the increasing rate of teenage pregnancy, affect children. In addition to the annual newsletter Facts at a Glance, which presents the latest data on teen pregnancy rates for every state, CT also publishes the papers "Next-Steps and Best Bets: Approaches to Preventing Adolescent Childbearing" and "Welfare and Adolescent Sex: The Effects of Family History, Benefit Levels," and "Community Context."

Concerned Women for America (CWA)
370 L'Enfant Promenade SW, Suite 800
Washington, DC 20024
202/488-7000
fax: 202/488-0806
website: http://www.cwfa.org/

CWA's purpose is to preserve, protect, and promote traditional Judeo-Christian values through education, legislative action, and other activities. It is concerned with creating an environment that is conducive to building strong families and raising healthy children. CWA publishes the monthly *Family Voice*, which periodically addresses issues such as abortion and promoting sexual abstinence in schools.

Family Research Council
700 13th St. NW, Suite 500
Washington, DC 20005
202/393-2100
fax: 202/393-2134
e-mail: corrdept@frc.org
website: http://www.frc.org

The council seeks to promote and protect the interests of the traditional family. It focuses on issues such as parental autonomy and responsibility, community support for single parents, and adolescent pregnancy. Among the council's numerous publications are the papers "Revolt of the Virgins," "Abstinence: The New Sexual Revolution," and "Abstinence Programs Show Promise in Reducing Sexual Activity and Pregnancy Among Teens."

Family Resource Coalition (FRC)
200 S. Michigan Ave., 16th Fl.
Chicago, IL 60604
312/341-0900
fax: 312/341-9361

The FRC is a national consulting and advocacy organization that seeks to strengthen and empower families and communities so they can foster the optimal development of children, teenagers, and adult family members. The FRC publishes the bimonthly newsletter *Connection*, the report "Family Involvement in Adolescent Pregnancy and Parenting Programs," and the fact sheet "Family Support Programs and Teen Parents."

Focus on the Family
8605 Explorer Dr.
Colorado Springs, CO 80995
719/531-3400; 800/A-FAMILY (232-6459)
fax: 719/548-4525
website: http://harvest.reapernet.com/fof/page18.html

Focus on the Family is a Christian organization dedicated to preserving and strengthening the traditional family. It believes that the breakdown of the traditional family is in part linked to increases in teen pregnancy, and it conducts research on the ethics of condom use and the effectiveness of safe-sex education programs in schools. The organization publishes the video "Sex, Lies, and . . . the Truth," which discusses the issue of teen sexuality and abstinence, as well as *Brio*, a monthly magazine for teenage girls.

Girls, Inc.
30 E. 33rd St.
New York, NY 10016-5394
212/689-3700
fax: 212/683-1253

Girls, Inc., is an organization for girls aged six to eighteen that works to create an environment in which girls can learn and grow to their full potential. It conducts daily programs in career and life planning, health and sexuality, and leadership and communication. Girls, Inc., publishes the newsletter *Girls Ink* six times a year, which provides information of interest to young girls and women, including information on teen pregnancy.

Heritage Foundation
214 Massachusetts Ave. NE
Washington, DC 20002-4999
202/546-4400
fax: 202/546-8328
e-mail: info@heritage.org
website: http://www.heritage.org

The Heritage Foundation is a public policy research institute that supports the ideas of limited government and the free-market system. It promotes the view that the welfare system has contributed to the problems of illegitimacy and teenage pregnancy. Among the foundation's numerous publications is its Backgrounder series, which includes "Liberal Welfare Programs: What the Data Show on Programs for Teenage Mothers"; the paper "Rising Illegitimacy: America's Social Catastrophe"; and the bulletin "How Congress Can Protect the Rights of Parents to Raise Their Children."

National Organization of Adolescent Pregnancy, Parenting, and Prevention (NOAPPP)
1319 F St. NW, Suite 401
Washington, DC 20004
202/783-5770
fax: 202/783-5775
e-mail: noappp@aol.com

NOAPPP promotes comprehensive and coordinated services designed for the prevention and resolution of problems associated with adolescent pregnancy and parenthood. It supports families in setting standards that encourage the healthy development of children through loving, stable relationships. NOAPPP publishes the quarterly *NOAPPP Network Newsletter* and various fact sheets on teen pregnancy.

Planned Parenthood Federation of America (PPFA)
810 Seventh Ave.
New York, NY 10019
212/541-7800
fax: 212/245-1845

PPFA is a national organization that supports people's right to make their own reproductive decisions without governmental interference. In 1989, it developed First Things First, a nationwide adolescent pregnancy prevention program. This program promotes the view that every child has the right to secure an education, attain physical and emotional maturity, and establish life goals before assuming the responsibilities of parenthood. Among PPFA's numerous publications are the booklets *Teen Sex?*, *Facts About Birth Control*, and *How to Talk with Your Teen About the Facts of Life*.

Progressive Policy Institute (PPI)
518 C St. NE
Washington, DC 20002
202/547-0001
fax: 202/544-5014
website: http://www.dlcppi.org

The PPI is a public policy research organization that strives to develop alternatives to the traditional debate between the left and the right. It advocates economic policies designed to stimulate broad upward mobility and social policies designed to liberate the poor from poverty and dependence. The institute publishes *Reducing Teenage Pregnancy: A Handbook for Action* and the reports "Second-Chance Homes: Breaking the Cycle of Teen Pregnancy" and "Preventable Calamity: Rolling Back Teen Pregnancy."

Religious Coalition for Reproductive Choice
1025 Vermont Ave. NW, Suite 1130
Washington, DC 20005
202/628-7700
fax: 202/628-7716

The coalition works to inform the media and the public that many mainstream religions support reproductive options, including abortion, and oppose antiabortion violence. It works to mobilize pro-choice religious people to counsel families facing unintended pregnancies. The coalition publishes "The Role of Religious Congregations in Fostering Adolescent Sexual Health," "Abortion: Finding Your Own Truth," and "Considering Abortion? Clarify What You Believe."

Robin Hood Foundation
111 Broadway, 19th Fl.
New York, NY 10006

212/227-6601
fax: 212/227-6698

The Robin Hood Foundation funds and provides technical assistance to organizations serving New Yorkers with very low incomes. The foundation makes grants to early childhood, youth, and family-centered programs located in the five boroughs of New York City. It publishes the report "Kids Having Kids: A Robin Hood Foundation Special Report on the Costs of Adolescent Childbearing."

**Sexuality Information and Education
Council of the U.S. (SIECUS)**
130 W. 42nd St., Suite 350
New York, NY 10036-7802
212/819-9770
fax: 212/819-9776
e-mail: SIECUS@siecus.org

SIECUS develops, collects, and disseminates information on human sexuality. It promotes comprehensive education about sexuality and advocates the right of individuals to make responsible sexual choices. In addition to providing guidelines for sexuality education for kindergarten through twelfth grades, SIECUS publishes the reports "Facing Facts: Sexual Health for America's Adolescents" and "Teens Talk About Sex: Adolescent Sexuality in the 90s" and the fact sheet "Adolescents and Abstinence."

**Teen STAR Program
Natural Family Planning Center of Washington, D.C.**
8514 Bradmoor Dr.,
Bethesda, MD 20817-3810
301/897-9323
fax: 301/571-5267

Teen STAR (Sexuality Teaching in the context of Adult Responsibility) is geared for early, middle, and late adolescence. Classes are designed to foster understanding of the body and its fertility pattern and to explore the emotional, cognitive, social, and spiritual aspects of human sexuality. Teen STAR publishes a bimonthly newsletter and the paper "Sexual Behavior of Youth: How to Influence It."

FOR FURTHER READING

Joan Jacobs Brumberg, *The Body Project: An Intimate History of American Girls*. New York: Random House, 1997. An intriguing portrait of teenage girls in American society.

Robert Coles, with Robert E. Coles, Daniel A. Coles, and Michael H. Coles, *The Youngest Parents: Teenage Pregnancy as It Shapes Lives*. New York: W.W. Norton, 1997. A depiction of the lives of young parents living throughout America, complete with photographs.

Mary Pipher, *Reviving Ophelia: Saving the Selves of Adolescent Girls*. New York: Ballantine Books, 1994. An insightful examination of the struggles that adolescent girls undergo in American society and how these struggles make them susceptible to depression, substance abuse, and pregnancy.

WORKS CONSULTED

Books

Kathleen Mullan Harris, *Teen Mothers and the Revolving Welfare Door*. Philadelphia: Temple University Press, 1997. An examination of the impact of teen motherhood on society, especially as it relates to welfare and other public assistance programs.

Elaine Bell Kaplan, *Not Our Kind of Girl: Unraveling the Myths of Black Teenage Motherhood*. Los Angeles: University of California Press, 1997. A sophisticated discussion of the causes of teen pregnancy in African American communities. Kaplan's thoughtful conclusions are based on her extensive interviews with teen mothers.

Kristin Luker, *Dubious Conceptions: The Politics of Teen Pregnancy*. Cambridge, MA: Harvard University Press, 1996. A scholarly but accessible analysis of the causes of teen pregnancy and the political forces that shape society's perception and treatment of teen mothers.

Rebecca A. Maynard, ed., *Kids Having Kids: Economic Costs and Social Consequences of Teen Pregnancy*. Washington, DC: Urban Institute Press, 1997. A study of the costs of teenage pregnancy on society, in terms of economics and social problems such as crime.

Stephen P. Thompson, ed., *Teen Pregnancy: Opposing Viewpoints*. San Diego: Greenhaven Press, 1997. An anthology that offers multiple perspectives on the causes of teen pregnancy, the effectiveness of various prevention measures, and the need for new initiatives to reduce teen pregnancy.

Periodicals and Websites

Adoptive Families, November/December 1998.

Tammy Busche, "Young People Commit to Sexual Purity as Part of 'True Love Waits' Campaign," *St. Charles County Post*, March 19, 1999.

Michael A. Carrera, "Preventing Adolescent Pregnancy: In Hot Pursuit," *Siecus Report*, August/September 1995.

Linda Chavez, "Ironically, a Drop in Teen Sex Comes at a Time When Many Adults Have Given Up Trying to Preach Abstinence," *Enterprise/Salt Lake City*, February 15, 1999.

Richard Cohen, "Sex-Is-Shameful Attitude," *Liberal Opinion Week*, July 5, 1997.

E.J. Dionne, "An Argument for Abstinence-Plus," *Denver Post*, July 16, 1999.

Education Digest, "Curricular Programs to Curb Teen Pregnancy," March 1999.

Barbara Ehrenreich, "Where Have All the Babies Gone?" *Life*, January 1998.

Joycelyn Elders, "Adolescent Pregnancy and Sexual Abuse," *Journal of the American Medical Association*, August 19, 1998.

Patrick F. Fagan, "Out of Wedlock Pregnancy: Derailing the Future Generation." Testimony before the House Subcommittee on Empowerment, July 16, 1998.

Lisa Fernandez, "Cut Sought in Latina Teen Births," *San Francisco Chronicle*, February 9, 1999.

Trisha Flynn, "Attitude Plus Access Equals Success," *Denver Post*, June 6, 1999.

Fawn Germer, "Babies Are Grown-Up Reality," *Tampa Tribune*, December 13, 1998.

Debra W. Haffner, "Are Abstinence-Only Sex-Education Programs Good for Teenagers? No: Abstinence-Only Education Isn't Enough. Teens Need a Wide Range of Information," *Insight*, September 29, 1997.

Molly Ivins, "Teen Mothers Lack Good Role Models," *Liberal Opinion Week*, September 22, 1997.

Janine Jackson, "The 'Crisis' of Teen Pregnancy: Girls Pay the Price for Media Distortion," *Extra!* March/April 1994.

Douglas Kirby, "Reflections on Two Decades of Research on Teen Sexual Behavior and Pregnancy," *Journal of School Health*, March 1999.

Sharon Lerner, "Just Say No to Sex; Just Say Yes to Big Bucks," *Salon Magazine*, September 23, 1999. On-line. Internet. Available at http://www.salonmagazine.com/health/feature/1999/09/23/abstinence/index.html.

Mike Males, "Adult Partners and Adult Contexts of 'Teenage Sex,'" *Education and Urban Society*, February 1998.

Mike Males, "In Defense of Teenaged Mothers," *Progressive*, August 1994.

Joe S. McIlhaney Jr., "Q: Are Abstinence-Only Sex-Education Programs Good for Children? Yes: 'Safe Sex' Education Has Failed. It's Time to Give Kids the Good News About Abstinence," *Insight*, September 29, 1997.

Mary A. Mitchell, "Pregnant? No Problem," *Chicago Sun-Times*, June 11, 1998.

Charles Murray, "The Coming White Underclass," *Wall Street Journal*, October 29, 1993.

National Campaign to Prevent Teen Pregnancy, "Teens Comment On." On-line. Internet. Available at http://www.teenpregnancy.org/teen/teenrent.htm.

National Coalition for Abstinence Education, "Frequently Asked Questions About the Title V Abstinence Education Program." On-line. Internet. Available at http://www.family.org/cforum/hptissues/A0001033.html.

Leonard Pitts Jr., "It's Time for Older Men Who Impregnate Girls to Grow Up," *Houston Chronicle*, March 5, 1999.

Kathryn Simpson, "Teen Pregnancy Affects All of Us: Young Moms Unready for Life's Stresses," *Arizona Republic*, January 13, 1999.

Gary Thomas, "Where True Love Waits," *Christianity Today*, March 1, 1999.

Steve Trombley, "Sex Education Helps Cut Teen Pregnancies," *Chicago Sun-Times*, May 7, 1999.

United States Code Annotated Title 42. The Public Health and Welfare. On-line. Internet. Available at http://www.tdh.texas.gov/abstain/federal.htm.

Cheryl Wetzstein, "Teaching Abstinence in Schools," *Insight*, September 22, 1997.

Barbara Dafoe Whitehead, "Dan Quayle Was Right," *Atlantic Monthly*, April 1993.

David Whitman, Paul Glastris, and Brendan I. Koener, "Was It Good for Us?" *U.S. News & World Report*, May 19, 1997.

Pat Wingert, "The Battle Over Falling Birth Rates," *Newsweek*, May 11, 1998.

Renee Wixon, "Instead of Condoms, Let's Give Teens Help in Abstaining From Sex," *Star Tribune*, April 3, 1999.

Sue Woodman, "How Teen Pregnancy Has Become a Political Football," *Ms.*, January/February 1995.

Sarah Yang, "Teen Pregnancy Programs Begin to Target Males," *Los Angeles Times,* June 24, 1999.

Reports

Hearings on the Social and Economic Costs of Teen Pregnancy Before the Empowerment Subcommittee of the Small Business Committee. Washington, DC: U.S. Government Printing Office, 1998.

Douglas Kirby, *No Easy Answers: Research Findings on Programs to Reduce Teen Pregnancy.* Washington, DC: National Campaign to Prevent Teen Pregnancy, 1997.

National Campaign to Prevent Teen Pregnancy, *What About the Teens? Research on What Teens Say About Teen Pregnancy: A Focus Group Report.* Washington, DC, 1999.

National Campaign to Prevent Teen Pregnancy, *Where Are the Adults? A Focus Group Report.* Washington, DC, 1998.

National Campaign to Prevent Teen Pregnancy, *While the Adults Are Arguing, the Teens Are Getting Pregnant: Overcoming Conflict in Teen Pregnancy Prevention.* Washington, DC, 1998.

Barbara Dafoe Whitehead and Theodora Ooms, *Goodbye to Girlhood: What's Troubling Girls and What Can We Do About It?* Washington, DC: National Campaign to Prevent Teen Pregnancy, 1999.

INDEX

abortion rates, 57
abstinence movement
  does not reduce sexual activity, 59
  increases teen pregnancy, 59–60
  is unrealistic, 61
  true agenda of, 59
  type of teens who practice, 52–53
  will reduce teen pregnancy, 52–54, 56
"abstinence-plus," 60
Adoptive Families (journal), 13
adult men, exploitation by, 42–44
advertising
  and sexuality, 47–48
African Americans, teen pregnancy rates of,
  17, 57
AIDS
  fear of, 52
  and premarital sex, 8, 55
Alan Guttmacher Institute, 6, 17, 58

babies, of teen mothers, 12
beauty industry, 48
birth control
  abstinence movement views on, 60
  access to, 34
  arguments for not teaching, 60
  cannot protect against diseases, 56
  failure rate of, 55–56
  fears about, 39
  increase in use of, 57–58
  ineffectiveness of, 56
  is lowering teen pregnancy rates, 57–58,
    60–61
  lack of education about, 58
  reasons for not using, 49
Blum, Robert, 57
boyfriends, abandoning pregnant
  girlfriends, 23

California
  abstinence programs in, 59
  rape laws in, 44–45
careers
  for disadvantaged teens, 35
  for uneducated teens, 33
Carrera, Michael A., 34
causes of teen pregnancy
  abstinence movement, 59–60
  are overlooked by politicians, 19–20
  being raised in poverty, 32–34
  belief that babies improve life, 34–35
  comprehensive sex education, 54–56
  cultural pressures, 46–48

exploitation by adult men, 42–44
feelings of hopelessness, 33–34
glamorous image of teen mothers,
  63–64
lack of
  parental guidance, 37–41
  social stigma, 63–64
sexual abuse by men, 44
sexual revolution, 63–64
Chavez, Linda, 40, 41
Chicago Sun-Times (newspaper), 62
child abuse
  by teen mothers, 15
  of pregnant teens, 29–30
child care centers, at schools, 64
child neglect, by teen mothers, 15
children, of teen mothers
  abuse and neglect of, 15
  become teen parents themselves, 15–16,
    38
  daily responsibility for, 25
  developmental problems of, 14
  expense of, 23–24, 35
  health risks faced by, 12
  statistics on, 15, 16, 38
  troubled futures of, 15
chlamydia, 56
Christianity Today (magazine), 53
Cohen, Richard, 8
Cole, Robert, 34
comprehensive sex education
  creates illusion of safe sex, 55–56
  defective logic of, 54–55
  does not encourage premarital sex, 60
  increases teen pregnancy rates, 54–56
  purpose of, 9
condoms
  are lowering teen pregnancy rates, 57–58
  cannot protect against diseases, 56
  failure rate of, 55–56
  increase in use of, 57–58
  ineffectiveness of, 56
Consortium of State Physicians Resource
  Councils, 53
contraception
  abstinence movements, views on, 60
  access to, 34
  arguments for not teaching, 60
  cannot protect against diseases, 56
  failure rate of, 55–56
  fears about, 39
  increase in use of, 57–58
  ineffectiveness of, 56

92

ABOUT THE AUTHOR

Jennifer A. Hurley is a book editor for Greenhaven Press and a part-time English instructor at the University of Phoenix and National University. She has a master's degree in Creative Writing from Boston University and continues to write fiction.